NEFERTITI'S FACE

NEFERTITI'S FACE

THE CREATION OF AN ICON

JOYCE TYLDESLEY

P

PROFILE BOOKS

For all my students, past, present and future.

First published in Great Britain in 2018 by
PROFILE BOOKS LTD
3 Holford Yard
Bevin Way
London WC1X 9HD
www.profilebooks.com

1 3 5 7 9 10 8 6 4 2

Typeset in Adobe Garamond by MacGuru Ltd
Printed and bound in Great Britain by
Clays Ltd, St Ives plc

A CIP catalogue record for this book is available from the British Library.

ISBN 978 1 78125 050 1
eISBN 978 1 84765 890 6

CONTENTS

ACKNOWLEDGEMENTS

I always worry when I start a new book. Is my subject of interest to a wide readership or – horrible thought – is it simply my own, self-indulgent obsession? With this book, all worries soon evaporated. The 'Berlin bust' which is believed to depict Queen Nefertiti is clearly a subject of interest to many people, and from the outset I have been overwhelmed by the support that I have received from friends, colleagues, students and complete strangers too numerous to mention individually. Thank you all.

The themes developed in this book were first presented in a lecture given to the Egypt Exploration Society in 2010, and refined for a lecture given for the Showcase Seminar series in the Manchester Museum in 2011. I would like to thank both organisations for their support. The delay in writing was caused by an unfortunate series of personal circumstances. I would like to thank all my editors at Profile Books – the late Peter Carson, Daniel Crewe, Penny Daniel and Cecily Gayford – as well as my copy-editor, Trevor Horwood, for their patience with what must, at times, have seemed like a never-ending project.

Campbell Price, Curator of Egypt and Sudan at the Manchester Museum, never allowed me to give up on Nefertiti. Carolyn Routledge and Angela Thomas, both former Curators of Egyptology and

Archaeology at Bolton Museum, each provided helpful information about the Bolton Nefertiti replica. George Rothschild has generously taken the time to discuss his great uncle, Ludwig Borchardt, with me. 'Michelle', of Southern Artists, Forgers and Hackers, has discussed the creation of the Landis replica bust and Cosmo Wenman has shared his work on the Nefertiti 3D scan heist/hoax. Pauline Norris explained the importance of Thutmose's horse blinker. Amanda Turnbull shared both her art and her library; Joseph Thimes shared his knowledge of DNA; and Dominique Leroux shared the fortuitous finding of a replica Nefertiti in Paris. Robin Snell explained the importance of her Nefertiti tattoo, while Kerry Webb provided random but important support, from thoughts on bald Disney villainesses to links to articles and television programmes, and encouraged me with a series of cheerful postcards when I was on the verge of giving up. My family have gone to extraordinary lengths to support my growing obsession with the Nefertiti bust. In particular my brother, Frank Tyldesley, volunteered (or was volunteered) to make a life-sized limestone replica, just so that I could get some idea of how the original might have been made. My husband, Steven Snape, supported me through my writing and accompanied me to many museums and art galleries on my quest to look at as many different forms of Nefertiti as possible. I am grateful to them all.

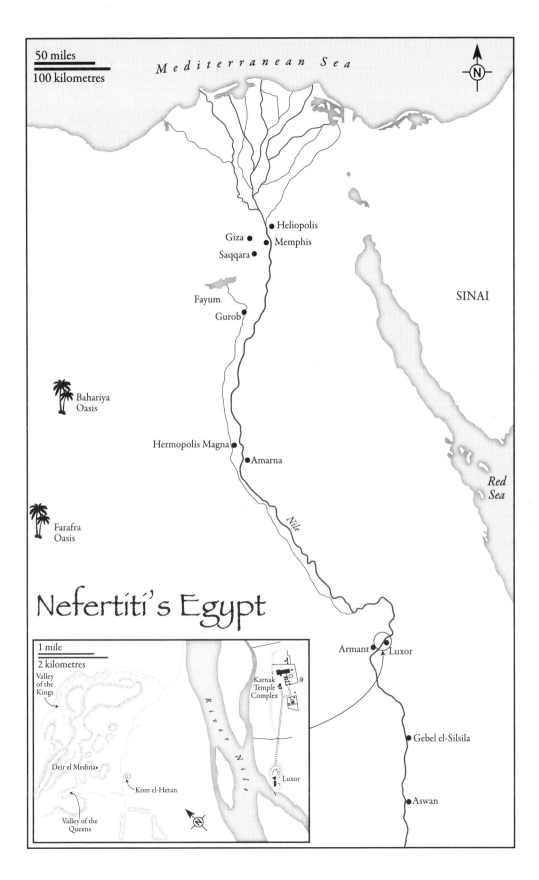

50 miles
100 kilometres

Mediterranean Sea

SINAI

● Heliopolis
Giza ● ●) Memphis
Saqqara ●

Fayum
Gurob ●

Bahariya
Oasis

Farafra
Oasis

Hermopolis Magna ●
● Amarna

Nile

Red
Sea

Nefertiti's Egypt

1 mile
2 kilometres

Valley
of the
Kings

Armant ● ●) Luxor

Karnak
Temple
Complex

River Nile

Deir el Medina ●

Kom el-Hetan

Luxor

● Gebel el-Silsila

Valley of the
Queens

● Aswan

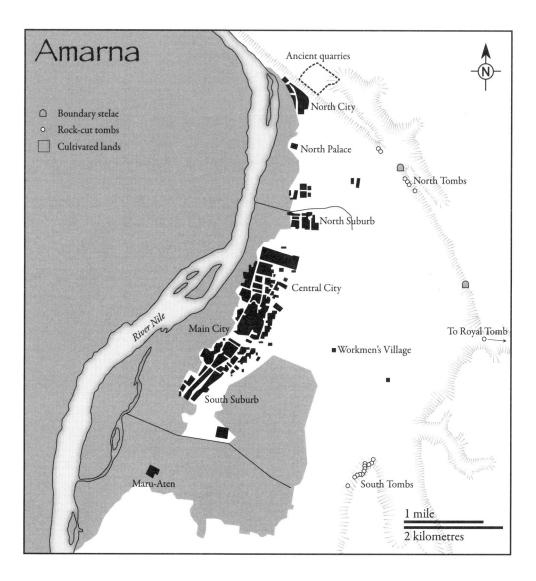

Amarna

Ancient quarries

North City

North Palace

North Tombs

North Suburb

Central City

Main City

To Royal Tomb

Workmen's Village

South Suburb

Maru-Aten

South Tombs

River Nile

⌂ Boundary stelae
○ Rock-cut tombs
▢ Cultivated lands

N

1 mile
2 kilometres

Thutmose's House/Workshop

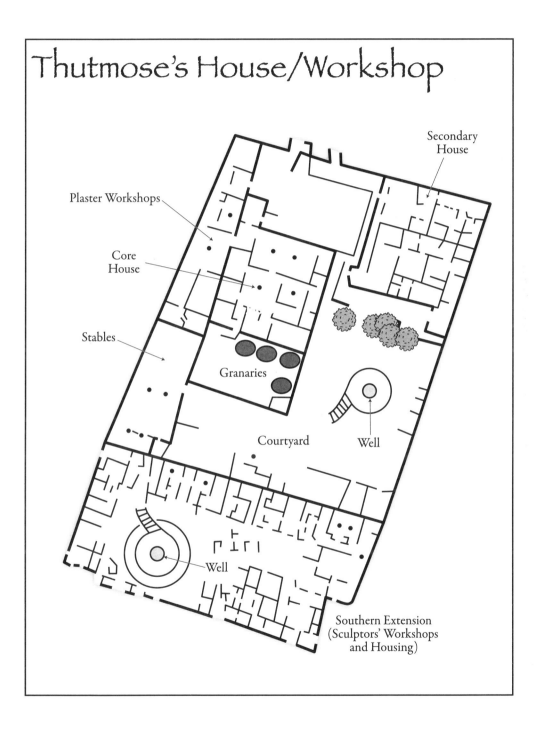

Secondary House

Plaster Workshops

Core House

Stables

Granaries

Courtyard

Well

Well

Southern Extension
(Sculptors' Workshops
and Housing)

INTRODUCTION:
SEEKING NEFERTITI

One of the most interesting features of modern historical work is the attempt of the historian, not only to construct a complete and reliable skeleton of fact about particular peoples and periods, but also, when that has been done, to clothe the dry bones with flesh and blood, and to inspire them with life and movement. The dry catalogues of events and dynasties which served as histories in the past no longer satisfy us. We wish to know how people lived, acted, thought, in ancient days, to see them as they wrought their day's work, to follow them into the intimacies of their homes, to know what they believed in and hoped for, even what amused them in their hours of relaxation. Perhaps even more keenly do we desire to realise individual personality, where such a thing is possible, and to be able to form in our own minds an actual conception of the men who made history in the past.

James Baikie (1929)[1]

As a child, I loved the gloomy Egyptian gallery in Bolton Museum.

Here, hidden amongst the countless dusty pots, could be found a whole treasury of wonders: the Rosetta Stone, a partially unwrapped female mummy lying in a decorated coffin, a squat Peruvian mummy sewn into what looked like a sack, and the sculpted head of a beautiful woman named Nefertiti. I don't know how old I was when I realised that not everything on display was quite what it seemed. The Rosetta Stone was – much to my indignation – a reproduction of the original, which has long been a key piece in the British Museum's collection. The Egyptian mummy was genuinely ancient, but would later be reclassified as a man while its decorated coffin remained that of a woman; a useful reminder that not every dead Egyptian made the long journey to Lancashire with his or her own accessories. Nefertiti's head was less than a century old; a plaster copy of a bust then on display in West Berlin, and just one of a host of identical plaster Nefertitis confusing children and their parents in museums throughout the Western world. Only the Peruvian mummy – the inexplicable and, to me, sinister intruder in the Egyptian gallery – was exactly what it appeared to be.

The Bolton Nefertiti, then, was a fake or, as the museum would probably prefer to classify it, a replica. Fake or real: this did not matter to the young me. The bust was a beautiful object in its own right, and my fascination with Nefertiti had been born. Twenty-five years later this fascination led me to write a book about Nefertiti.[2] I set out full of enthusiasm to create a fat, fact-packed biography of Egypt's sun queen, but soon realised that this would never be possible. Nefertiti's life is preserved in pictures rather than words, and the undisputed facts can be condensed into a very short list. We know that she was the consort of the Eighteenth Dynasty king Akhenaten (formerly known as Amenhotep IV), who ruled Egypt at a time of unprecedented wealth and empire. We know that she lived most of her adult life at the new royal city of Amarna, and that she bore her husband at least six daughters. We know that she was allocated a prominent role in Akhenaten's solar cult, and that she often wore a unique flat-topped crown while performing her religious and political duties. We know that she fades from our view at the end of her husband's reign. And that is more or less it. Alongside these facts, we have many areas of conjecture. Who were Nefertiti's parents? Was she worshipped as a living goddess? Did her son inherit the Egyptian throne? We are particularly intrigued by her disappearance, which seems somehow inappropriate and unconvincing for such a prominent woman. Could she really have died and been buried during her husband's reign? Or could she have moved on, perhaps changing her name and role to continue her career trajectory?

This lack of personal information is far from unusual. Three thousand years of dynastic history have yielded the names of many hundreds of queens, but we know very little about the private lives of any of these remote ladies. Births, marriages and deaths were not routinely commemorated in the monumental inscriptions that would have made them accessible to us today and, although we may have a splendid if empty tomb to stand as testament to a magnificent funeral and – maybe – a loving husband or son, death for the most part went unrecorded too. The best-recorded queens are those who were born into the royal family and who outlived their husbands to become the mothers of kings, but even these women are frustratingly ill documented. So it is not sinister, mysterious or meaningful that we know so little about Nefertiti's life and, in particular, about her death and burial. The deafening silence does not necessarily conceal a plot twist, however much we might hope for one.

However, it does leave us wanting to know more about Nefertiti, and her role in the Amarna drama. This is a relatively recent development. At the turn of the last century no account of the Amarna Period would have cast Nefertiti in the central female role. Her name and her awkward gawkiness survived in imagery and sculpture, but she was a minor character in comparison to her formidable mother-in-law, Queen Tiy. Tiy, it was accepted, developed the role of the politically active consort and queen mother, with Nefertiti merely following her lead. Few, in fact, would have been interested in either Tiy or Nefertiti. The Amarna Period was very much a niche subject, of interest mainly to biblical scholars vainly seeking a means of linking the 'heretic' Akhenaten to Moses. This started to change when, in 1911, a German expedition directed by Ludwig Borchardt began to excavate the ruined city of Amarna. The first exhibition of finds from the site drew large crowds to Berlin's Neues Museum and sparked an excitement which only increased when, in 1922, Howard Carter discovered Tutankhamen's near-intact tomb in the Valley of the Kings.[3]

Tutankhamen was a British archaeological triumph that caused the other excavating nations to grind their teeth in frustration. It is perhaps no coincidence that, within months of the discovery, a colourfully painted life-sized portrait bust was unveiled in the Neues Museum. The bust depicted a beautiful and startlingly lifelike Egyptian queen with a smooth pink-brown skin, deeper red-brown lips, a straight nose and arched black brows. She was unlabelled, but wore the flat-topped blue crown which was unique to Nefertiti, mother-in-law – and possibly also mother – of the celebrity of the day. Nefertiti's bust fitted perfectly with the colourful, geometric art deco style that was starting to represent post-war opulence and glamour. It could easily have been sculpted by Demétre Chiparus or Ferdinand Preiss, yet it was the creation of a sculptor who had lived and died several thousands of years earlier. Ample publicity ensured that long queues of admirers arrived daily at the Neues Museum. This, of course, resulted in yet more publicity and even longer queues until, like many modern celebrities, the Berlin bust and, by extension, Nefertiti herself had become famous simply for being famous. Germany, a land so recently stripped of its royalty, had acquired a new queen and, as Nefertiti's fame was extrapolated backwards, Tiy was forced to abdicate her role as the foremost queen of the Amarna court.

All other portraits forgotten, the Berlin bust quickly became the one and only version of Nefertiti. While Tutankhamen remained frustratingly invisible, sealed in his nest of coffins in the Valley of the Kings, replica Nefertitis travelled the Western world. Soon she existed, simultaneously, in increasing numbers of museum galleries and – executed with varying degrees of accuracy, as copies were made of the official replicas, only to be themselves copied – was available from increasing numbers of outlets. By 1925 a replica Nefertiti bust had reached Bolton, where she was (and still is) featured alongside a mixture of genuine and reproduction artefacts recovered from Amarna. It was entirely predictable that the bust would quickly become the subject of highest-level diplomatic discussion, with the Egyptian authorities demanding that their 'stolen property' be repatriated and the German authorities defending their ownership of a 'legally acquired artefact'. It was equally predictable that it would become the subject of many and varied conspiracy theories: exactly when, where and by whom had it been made?

Ancient Egypt has yielded more than its fair share of artistic masterpieces, but it is difficult to think of another sculpture that has so successfully bridged the gap between the ancient and modern worlds. The timeless beauty of the Berlin Nefertiti both attracts us and sparks our imagination, but in so doing it obscures our view of the past, shifting attention not only from the other members of the Amarna court, but also from other, equally valid, representations of Nefertiti herself. At the same time, the bust's very familiarity clouds our view, making it difficult for us to see what is actually before our eyes. In this book I set out to explore the creation of a cultural icon. I have divided the book into two parts. The first, 'Creating

Nefertiti', returns the bust to its original context by considering the evidence for its creator, its manufacture and its purpose. Part II, 'Recreating Nefertiti', sets the bust in its modern context by discussing its discovery, its display and its dual role as a political pawn and artistic inspiration. In order to make sense of the Egyptian history underpinning the story of the bust, I begin with a brief introduction to Nefertiti's life and times. To bring things up to date, I end by considering the most recent attempts to trace Nefertiti's remains. The endnotes numbered throughout the text will allow the more curious reader to discover further details about Nefertiti and her images.

BACKGROUND TO THE AMARNA AGE

The Tel el-Amarna period has had more nonsense written about it than any other period in Egyptian history.

Margaret Murray (1949)[1]

More than 3,000 years ago an Egyptian sculptor created an artistic masterpiece. This book focuses on the conception, creation, replication and dissemination of that masterpiece: a plastered and colourfully painted bust of Queen Nefertiti, which is currently on display in the Neues Museum, home of Berlin's Egyptian Museum and Papyrus Collection.[2] However, no artefact should be studied in isolation. This brief section provides the background information necessary to view the bust, its creator(s) and its subject in their proper context.[3] If it seems to focus on Akhenaten rather than on the bust, its creator, or Nefertiti herself, this is unavoidable. Akhenaten was the king of Egypt and, as such, had no living equal. His word was law, and his decision to worship one particular god had a major impact on everything and everyone – queen, art and artists included

– around him. It is only by understanding this that we can start to gain an understanding of Amarna life and art.

Nefertiti was the consort of the king, or pharaoh, Akhenaten, who came to the throne as Amenhotep IV. Akhenaten ruled Late Bronze Age Egypt towards the end of the Eighteenth Dynasty. The kings of the later Eighteenth Dynasty, and their reign lengths, are conventionally listed as follows:

Tuthmosis IV 1400–1390 BCE

Amenhotep III 1390–1352 BCE

Amenhotep IV, who subsequently changed his name to Akhenaten, 1352–1336 BCE

Smenkhkare 1338–1336 BCE

Tutankhaten, who subsequently changed his name to Tutankhamen, 1336–1327 BCE

Ay 1327–1323 BCE

Horemheb 1323–1295 BCE.[4]

All these dates are approximate. Although the Egyptians maintained long chronological lists of their kings, they did not use a linear calendar to date events. They saw time as an endlessly repeating cycle of reigns and so, when a king died, time began again with a new king – the continuation of all kings who had gone before – and a new year 1. This system has been adopted by Egyptologists because, although it is by no means perfect, it is the most accurate means that we have of dating specific events. When we state that

Nefertiti's husband swore an oath of dedication to establish the limits of a new royal city in his regnal year 6, we know exactly what we mean. We struggle, however, to tie this dedication to a specific calendar year. Unfortunately this traditional Egyptocentric dating method can appear baffling to non-Egyptologists and, as it isolates Egypt from the rest of the ancient world, has added to the air of mystery that is so often, and so unnecessarily, associated with the dynastic age.

Nefertiti's own timeline is best documented with reference to her husband's regnal years as follows:

Year 1: Nefertiti becomes Akhenaten's consort. The date of their marriage is unknown. Nefertiti's parentage is unexplained. Daughter Meritaten is born by the end of year 1.

Year 2: New building works at Thebes include the Benben Temple (*Hwt bnbn*), a temple that features Nefertiti in the role of priest. Nefertiti receives an extended name, becoming Neferneferuaten – Nefertiti 'Exquisite Beauty of the Aten. A Beautiful Woman has Come'.

Year 3: Akhenaten's *heb-sed* jubilee is celebrated at Thebes. Nefertiti plays an obvious role in the celebrations.

Year 4: Daughter Meketaten probably born this year.

Year 5: Building works start at Amarna.

Year 7: Daughter Ankhesenpaaten born before or during this year.

Year 8: Daughter Neferneferuaten-the-Younger born before or during this year.

Year 9: The royal family has made a permanent move to Amarna. Daughters Neferneferure and Setepenre are born before the end of this year.

Year 12: Nefertiti's bust is carved this year or later, in

Thutmose's workshop. Nefertiti, Akhenaten and all six
daughters attend an international festival at Amarna.

Year 13(?): A scene in the royal tomb depicts Nefertiti
mourning the death of Meketaten.

Year 16: A graffito in a quarry near Amarna refers to
Nefertiti as Akhenaten's consort. Our last
contemporary sighting of the queen.

Nefertiti was not her husband's only wife. Like all of Egypt's
kings, Akhenaten maintained a harem of secondary queens of
varying status. Traditionally the royal wives might include the
daughters of Egyptian kings and the daughters of brother-kings and
foreign vessels sent to Egypt to participate in the diplomatic marriages which linked the Egyptian empire together. Living alongside
his wives, although not necessarily permanent harem residents, were
Akhenaten's unmarried female dependants, his widowed mother,
sisters, aunts, and the wives inherited from his dead father, plus their
children, servants and attendants. Together they formed a strong,
economically independent, female-based community.

As consort, or 'King's Great Wife', Nefertiti enjoyed a very different life from her co-wives. She lived in the palace, not the harem,
where she was recognised as the mother in the nuclear royal family.
She was the queen who, bearing the appropriate titles, crowns and
regalia, was represented in all official writings and artwork. If all
went to plan her son would eventually inherit his father's crown,
allowing Nefertiti to progress to the highly respected role of King's
Mother. The consort was, however, far more than a baby machine.
She was an essential element in the monarchy and, like any good
Egyptian wife, she was expected to support her husband in all his
endeavours. Her political role is fairly clear to us; she was effectively
the king's deputy. In a time of crisis – a dead husband, for example
– she would rule Egypt until the next king was able to take his

rightful place on the throne. Her religious role is less easy for us to define, but we know that her responsibilities went far beyond observing routine rituals. The queen consort represented all of Egypt's women before the gods, while representing either all or one of the goddesses before the people. A consort married to a king who considered himself to be partially or wholly divine would herself, through proximity, become tinged with divinity.

A New City

Akhenaten was the head of Egypt's many cults, yet he chose to dedicate his life to just one god: an ancient but hitherto unimportant solar deity known simply as the Disc, or the Aten. Akhenaten's god represented the power of the sun, or the light of the sun, rather than the sun itself and, because the Aten was also associated with ideas of divine kingship, Akhenaten's god also admitted the possibility that the king and his immediate family might be living gods. This was a major break with tradition. Previously it had been understood that kings, although able to communicate with the gods and, in some cases, able to claim a god as a father, could become fully divine only after death. Many Egyptologists have wondered about Akhenaten's 'conversion': was it a true religious experience, or a cynical attempt to strip the existing priesthoods of their wealth and power by channelling all worship through the throne? We have no way of knowing, but this author believes it to have been entirely genuine.

Inspired by the Aten, Akhenaten built a new city. Here his god could be worshipped properly, without interference from any other state cult. Akhetaten (literally 'Horizon of the Aten') is today better known as Amarna. Taking its name from Akhenaten's new city, the Amarna Age (or Period) is the modern term applied to the time when Egypt was ruled from Amarna, and when its kings were devoted to the Aten. This includes most of the reign of Akhenaten, the entire reign of his mysterious co-regent and/or successor Smenkhkare, and the start of the reign of Tutankhaten, whose change of name to Tutankhamen signalled the end of the era.

Amarna was built on a virgin site on the east bank of the Nile and, isolated from the established administrative centres and their associated elite cemeteries, lay almost equidistant between Thebes to the south and Memphis to the north. A series of boundary markers, or stelae, defined the city limits; these extended across the river to include 'mountains, deserts, meadows, water, villages, embankments, men, beasts, groves and all things which the Aten shall bring into existence'. Several miles to the north-west of Amarna city, yet within the area defined by the boundary stelae, lay Hermopolis Magna (ancient Khmun; modern Ashmunein), a long-established town whose temple was dedicated to the god of wisdom, Thoth.

The massive stone pyramids of the Old Kingdom – each, through necessity, designed, built and substantially completed during a single reign – confirm that the Egyptians were no strangers to rapid building projects. The pharaohs had access to almost unlimited resources and their civil servants had honed the logistical skills needed to employ these resources effectively. Sun-dried mud-brick, the principal building material traditionally used in all domestic architecture and now, at Amarna, used in temple architecture too, was cheap and plentiful: mud could simply be scooped from the banks of the Nile, and several thousand bricks could easily be made in a day. Limestone, the 'soft' or sedimentary stone used in temple and royal architecture, was locally available and could be cut into small blocks in the quarry, for ease of transport and erection. This all contributed towards an almost unimaginably fast build. Construction started during year 5, and by year 9 Amarna was effectively complete, with temples, palaces, private housing, wells and, considered of utmost importance, statues in place. Superficially all looked splendid, but under the tiled and painted exteriors all was not well, and repairs would continue throughout the life of the city as the shoddy first-phase structures were improved or replaced.

Akhenaten moved eagerly to his new life in his new city, taking his family with him. Others – the civil servants who ran the empire, the craftsmen and artists who decorated the city, the labourers who built it, the servants who supported their masters and, of course, the priests who ensured that the Aten was worshipped effectively – sensed an exciting opportunity, and followed their king. At a conservative estimate, some 20,000 embarked on Akhenaten's great adventure, most of them relatively young men.[5] Parennefer, the royal butler, is the only official known to have followed Akhenaten from Thebes.

While his people seem to have been free to come and go as they pleased, Akhenaten took a personal vow never to leave his city. As far as we can see, he was true to his word. The days when the king travelled the length of the Nile to remind his subjects of his existence had ended; those who had royal business were now forced to travel to Amarna. Not even death would be allowed to separate Akhenaten from his beloved city and its god. As Amarna rose beside the river, a specialist group of workers started to create a royal tomb in a wadi, or dry river bed, in the eastern cliffs. To the north and south of the royal wadi, a series of rock-cut tombs would provide the Amarna elite with a suitable final resting place, and the deceased Akhenaten and his consort Nefertiti with an eternal court.

A New God

Egypt had always been a polytheistic land, happy to absorb new members into the pantheon. By the later Eighteenth Dynasty there were least 1,000 deities whose ability to change name, appearance and even character makes them impossible to count. These gods both controlled the living Egypt and offered the true-in-heart the chance of continued life beyond death. All were important, though some, the great state gods, were significantly more important than others. When Akhenaten came to the throne, the most powerful god of all was Amen, the 'hidden one' of Thebes. Amen was an ancient Theban deity, recently elevated to the position of state god by the Eighteenth Dynasty kings who credited him with their rise to power. Akhenaten's ancestors had vied with each other to make increasingly splendid improvements to Amen's Karnak Temple, which developed in complexity with every successive reign. The decision to create a royal cemetery in the Valley of the Kings, on the west bank of the Nile opposite the east bank Karnak Temple, was largely inspired by the desire to link the Eighteenth Dynasty kings forever with Amen.

While certain kings had favoured certain gods at certain times, none had obviously neglected their duty to all members of the pantheon. There was a sound practical reason for this. As the king was, in theory, the only Egyptian who could serve as a link between the people and their gods, he had the awesome responsibility of ensuring that the correct offerings were made in the state temples at the correct times. These offerings would reassure the gods that all was right within Egypt, and the gods would in turn allow Egypt to flourish. The concept of all being right within Egypt was known as *maat*, a word that denotes a combination of truth, 'rightness', justice and status quo. *Isfet*, or chaos, the opposite of *maat*, is easier for us to understand. Who knew what would happen if the offerings were not made, and the gods grew angry? Until now, no one had dared to find out. Akhenaten's decision to devote himself – and, as far as he could, his people – to just one god was a worrying development that threatened the security of the whole land.

Akhenaten was not a monotheist. He never denied the existence of Egypt's other gods and he remained comfortable with references to a range of solar deities, including Re and his daughter Maat, the personification of the concept *maat*. But if Re and his family were acceptable, Amen of Thebes was not. Akhenaten, it seems, hated Amen with a vengeance. In a very literal way, he set about erasing Amen from memory by closing his temples and attacking his name and image wherever he found them in official contexts. This persecution was so extreme that, during his reign, prominent individuals unlucky enough to bear names compounded with Amen (as indeed Amenhotep IV himself did) found it wise to adopt a new identity.

Our unavoidable focus on Amarna and the royal family throughout Akhenaten's reign makes it difficult to see what was happening in the wider Egypt at this time. But it seems that many of the traditional state temples were hastily converted into sun temples, with their priests quickly transferring their loyalty to the Aten. The extent to which this public purge affected private individuals is unclear. Certainly the Amarna elite had to be seen to follow their king's theology in life and in death. This is made clear both in their homes, where officially sanctioned images encouraged them to worship the Aten via the royal family, and in their tombs, where images of the Aten shining over the royal family replaced scenes of the old, comforting, funerary gods. With Osiris king of the dead banished, all possibility of entry to his afterlife kingdom had vanished, and Akhenaten's courtiers faced an eternity trapped in their rock-cut tombs. But in the walled village occupied by the specialist tomb builders, the situation was very different. Here the private chapels that the workmen built to honour their ancestors incorporated references to the traditional gods and included prayers addressed to Amen. Akhenaten's obsession may have forced the tomb builders to relocate to Amarna, but it did not cause them to abandon their fundamental beliefs.

The Experiment Ends

The Amarna Age ended early in the reign of Tutankhaten, when Akhenaten's experiment was officially and unequivocally rejected. Amarna was abandoned, the Aten demoted (but not banned), the traditional pantheon restored and the new king rebranded as Tutankhamen. Despite his very public change of image, Tutankhamen could never escape the fact that he had been born a member of the Amarna royal family while his short-lived successor, Ay, was known to have been a prominent member of the Amarna elite. Both were indelibly tainted with the 'Amarna heresy', and this did not endear them to their more orthodox successors. The Ramesside kings of the Nineteenth Dynasty (c.1295–1186 BCE) regarded Tutankhamen and Ay as inappropriate role models. Seeking to link their own arriviste family to Egypt's more ancient dynasties, the Ramessides recorded the names of all of Egypt's kings, providing one continuous line of 'ancestors' stretching from the mythical unifier of their land, Menes, to themselves. Akhenaten, Smenkhkare, Tutankhamen and Ay were omitted from their list so that Egypt's official history now moved seamlessly from Amenhotep III to Horemheb. Such was the magical power of the hieroglyphic word, the Amarna Period had never happened.

Akhenaten and his immediate successors were omitted from the works of the classical historians who preserved the greatly romanticised memories of many of Egypt's kings. Nor were they mentioned in the Bible, the only other reference available to early Egyptologists. Occasional tantalising tales – Herodotus, for example, mentions a king who closed the temples; Manetho tells a very confusing story of great upheaval at the end of the reign of Amenhotep III – suggest that Akhenaten's story may have survived in the oral tradition, but this was of little help to those who, following Jean-François Champollion's 1822 decoding of the hieroglyphic script, started to reconstruct Egypt's long history. None of the names mentioned in the newly discovered Amarna inscriptions could be tied into the king lists which formed the backbone of Egyptian history. It would take many years for the fragmented evidence for Akhenaten's reign to be joined into anything resembling a realistic history, and several key aspects of the Amarna Period are still the subject of fierce academic debate. No two Egyptologists interpret this period in exactly the same way. Because they developed only during the twentieth century, the myths that today envelop the Amarna royal family are entirely modern ones. Nefertiti, unlike her rival celebrity queen of Egypt, Cleopatra, is not burdened with the biases of the classical authors and Shakespeare.

Deserted first by the king and then by his people, Amarna started to deteriorate. As the mud-brick housing disintegrated into fertile soil it created a valuable resource that, over the centuries, has been collected and spread over neighbouring fields. The enterprising priests of Hermopolis Magna arrived to exploit Amarna's stone temples as quarries, collecting the ready-cut blocks and incorporating them in their own architecture. More calculated is the damage wrought during the reign of Horemheb, when a deliberate attempt was made to smash and efface the images of the royal family that once adorned the city. This vandalism stripped the surviving Amarna art of its immediate context and meaning, while destroying the inscriptions that might have helped us to understand the complexities of Akhenaten's religion. As a result, while we may understand how Amarna's art was created, we don't really understand how and by whom it was intended to be seen.

Aware of the threat posed by grave robbers in an unguarded royal cemetery, Tutankhamen had already returned to Amarna to empty the royal tomb and transport his family's remains to the Valley of the Kings. Within eight years of his visit, valuable grave goods 'rescued' from these Amarna burials would be recycled in his own tomb. While the royal and elite tombs were emptied, the ordinary people were forced to leave their dead behind. It is estimated that the Amarna desert cemeteries hold between 6,000 and 14,000 graves, many of which were robbed not long after the city was abandoned. Bones recovered from these graves betray the signs of a harsh life, with a poor diet and constant hard work leading, in many cases, to death at less than thirty-five years of age.

Excavating Amarna

Soon, Amarna had become a ghost city. No other king was tempted to occupy the Amarna plain and no substantial modern town ever developed, although there is evidence of sporadic late-Roman/Christian occupation, and a handful of modern villages have caused parts of the ancient settlement to disappear under cultivated fields. Centuries of dry conditions have ensured that the archaeology remains relatively intact, with many of the buildings surviving as foundations and low mud-brick walls, the taller walls, roofs and upper storeys having crumbled away. The brief lifespan of the city – no more than thirty years – means that the stratigraphy and dating of these buildings is relatively easy to interpret and so, following a century of near continuous excavation and publication, we know far more about the structure of Amarna, atypical though it undoubtedly is, than we do about any other dynastic city. The major work conducted at Amarna may be summarised as follows:

> **1714:** Father Claude Sicard becomes the first European to record details of a visit to Amarna; his publication includes a highly imaginative illustration of Amarna Boundary Stela A.

1798–9: Edme Jomard, a member of Napoleon's expedition, visits Amarna, noting 'a great mass of ruins'. His plan will be published in the *Description d'Égypte* in 1817.

1822: Champollion deciphers the hieroglyphic script. For the first time, it is possible to read the Amarna inscriptions.

1824 and 1826: John Gardner Wilkinson visits 'Alabastronopolis' and the nearby Hatnub quarry; he plans some of the elite tombs and publishes scenes from Meryre's tomb plus a sketch map of the site.

1843 and 1845: Karl Richard Lepsius and the Prussian Archaeological Mission explore the city in two brief seasons totalling just ten days, subsequently publishing a folio of drawings and a revised map.

1873: Amelia Edwards, author of *A Thousand Miles up the Nile*, includes Amarna in her list of important Middle Egyptian sites visited.

1880s: Gaston Maspero and Urbain Bourriant start to record the elite tombs. The royal tomb is discovered and emptied by locals, before being 'excavated' by Alessandro Barsanti.

1887: A local woman discovers the 'Amarna Letters'. Many are lost, the remainder are dispersed to various museum collections.

1891–2: Flinders Petrie surveys and partially excavates the Central City, assisted by Howard Carter.

1901–7: Norman de Garis Davies records and publishes the elite tombs and the boundary stelae.

1907, 1911–14: Ludwig Borchardt surveys then excavates much of the Main City for the Deutsche Orient-Gesellschaft. They discover the workshop of the sculptor Thutmose.

1921–1937: The Egypt Exploration Society conducts excavations directed by, amongst others, T. E. Peet, Leonard Woolley, Francis Newton, Henri Frankfort and John Pendlebury. In an exclusive deal with the EES, *The Illustrated London News* publicises the ongoing work at Amarna.

1960s: Occasional unpublished excavations by the Egyptian Antiquities Organisation.

1970s and 80s: Geoffrey Martin and Ali el-Khouly complete the recording and publication of the tombs in the Royal Wadi.

1977–present: Excavations directed by Barry Kemp, working successively with the Egypt Exploration Society, Cambridge University and the Amarna Trust.

Archaeology is destructive: the excavator has only one chance to get things right as, once dug, a site can never be restored. Fortunately, Amarna has attracted a series of competent excavators, all of whom worked to the highest standards of their time, and all of whom published their results. However, the standards of the past are not the standards that we expect of our archaeologists today. Many of the earlier excavators left areas within the houses unexcavated, and minor finds frequently went unrecorded. Indeed, their record keeping in general left something to be desired. As a result, it can be difficult to tie finds to specific buildings, or to specific rooms in those buildings. The current work, directed by Professor Kemp, is slowly but surely expanding our understanding of this remarkable city.

The Written Word

Alongside the archaeology, Amarna has provided us with a useful quantity of written material. This largely takes the form of monumental inscriptions and funerary texts; unfortunately, we lack the private writings and eyewitness accounts that would fully explain the complexities of life in Akhenaten's city.

Nefertiti and her family spoke the language that Egyptologists today call Late Egyptian. This was not, however, the language of the wider Mediterranean world. The correspondence that linked the kings, chiefs and vassals of the Near East was conducted in Akkadian, the language of Babylon, and diplomatic letters were inscribed in cuneiform wedges pressed into clay tablets. In 1887 the remains of the diplomatic archive were discovered at Amarna. The collection is incomplete, and the letters are difficult to translate and date.

Within Egypt, formal pronouncements and monumental inscriptions were written in the Late Egyptian language using the intricate but time-consuming hieroglyphic script. Less formal messages, also written in Late Egyptian, used the far speedier, cursive hieratic script. Although the spoken language consisted of both consonants and vowels, neither script recorded the vowels; the ancient scribes, practical as ever, saw no need to write the obvious. Those who could read the writings – no more than 10 per cent of the population and almost always male – automatically knew how the words were pronounced. This is a system that will be familiar to anyone who regularly sends and receives text messages.

Since Late Egyptian is no longer spoken, modern scribes have to take an educated guess which vowel goes where. Generally, 'e' is the vowel of choice, but this may not be the vowel that the Egyptians used, and we may not be inserting it in the correct place(s). As a result, all but the shortest Egyptian words – including personal and place names – have alternative English spellings, all equally valid. The situation is further confused by the tendency for Egyptologists to use Greek variants of Egyptian names. So, the sculptor who we will here call Thutmose (a personal name meaning '[the god] Thoth is born') bore exactly the same name as Nefertiti's grandfather-in-law Tuthmosis; acceptable variants of his name range from Thothmes to Djehutymose. The original Thoth was the divine scribe. In a land where words (hieroglyphic writing) took the form of images, he would always be linked to the carvings, painting and sculptures that could be read as words. Thutmose was therefore a highly appropriate name for any artist. The women whom I call Tiy (wife of Amenhotep III) and Tey (wife of Ay) actually bore the same name: I have chosen to use variant modern spellings to make the distinction between the two obvious.

We can, with reasonable confidence, translate the hieroglyphs. However, this does not mean that we can understand the full meaning of those ancient words. Different experts will translate the same text using different, equally valid, modern words, and their choices will affect our understanding. In a longer writing, this may not matter; the popular story of Sinuhe remains an action-packed adventure no matter who translates it. But when we want to understand precise titles and short messages it does matter. So, while we can see that Thutmose was described as a *s'ankh*, and we can understand that this can be translated as 'sculptor', we don't know what this title meant to his contemporaries. This becomes particularly important when we start to look for the evidence of Nefertiti's life and death, with complex scholarly arguments hanging on the precise interpretation of randomly preserved words and images.

We know a great deal about Amarna, its queen and her people. But it would be a huge mistake to think that we know and understand everything. There is still an enormous amount for us to learn.

PART I

CREATING NEFERTITI

Although in the matter of conception Egyptian art remains fixed and immovable in the archaic stage, there is nothing archaic in its actual execution. That is perfect. It is not the hand that is out. The practice of centuries in doing the same thing over and over again has trained this to complete ductility. It is the mind, the guiding intelligence, which should lead the way, and which among all progressive races does lead the way out of the archaic stage of development, which is at fault. This refuses to lead, and so for Egyptian art, no advance is possible ... Perfect yet primitive, young yet very old, its hoary infancy defies time. It is the image of routine, of the deadly monotony of unthinking iteration.

Lisle March Phillipps, writing in 1911,
before the discovery of Nefertiti's bust.[1]

The Egyptian portrait-sculptor is bit by bit gaining his rightful position as one of the great master-artists of the world – a position which a few years ago was scornfully denied him ...

Even on the evidence then extant, this [Lisle March Phillipps, quoted above] was an utterly unjustifiable criticism; but one imagines that so keen a judge of the beautiful would have made a speedy recantation of his heresy had he seen the wonderful series of heads which is now in the Berlin Museum ... Of these, the one in painted limestone has won world-wide recognition as one of the most exquisite of early sculptures in existence; and it well deserves its reputation.

James Baikie, writing in 1926, after the
public display of Nefertiti's bust.[2]

1

THUTMOSE

It is certain that the court of Akhenaten was a home and fostering ground of the arts.[1]

Norman de Garis Davies (1905)

Almost 3,500 years ago someone dropped a broken piece of inscribed ivory in a courtyard in the royal city of Amarna. When, on 17 December 1912, this fragment was recovered by a team of German Egyptologists led by Ludwig Borchardt, it was dismissed as an insignificant vessel cover. Only in 1983 was it recognised as a horse blinker.[2]

Blinkers, or blinders, are curved pieces of horse tack that are attached to a driving harness at each side of a horse's head in order to narrow the field of vision and prevent the animal from being spooked by the sight of a vehicle approaching from behind. In ancient Egypt, blinkers were designed to keep the chariot horse's attention on its job. Scenes of horses and chariots carved on temple and tomb walls show that the blinkers were fitted so that the eyes of the horse were visible, suggesting that they specifically shielded the horse's view of the driver in the chariot behind.[3] He would be standing above and behind the horse; this is something that horses dislike, and which will cause them to bolt. Relatively rare in Eighteenth Dynasty Egypt – as, indeed, were horses and their chariots – the blinkers recovered from this period are usually made from leather, wood or metal. Ivory is unusual and would have been very expensive; it seems probable that this blinker was made for royalty, either for their own use or to bestow as a gift.

Who was the privileged owner of this precious blinker, its horse and its pair and their associated chariot (and, presumably, charioteer)? Sadly, the hieroglyphic inscription is fractured, with only the upper part of the first line of text readable as 'the praised one of the Perfect God, the chief of works, the sculptor Thutmose'. It seems reasonable to conclude from this that the Thutmose in question once owned the blinker. The 'Perfect God', or 'Good God', is a title often used for the reigning king; given the find-spot, this is likely to be a king who ruled at Amarna. Akhenaten must be the clear favourite here, although Smenkhkare and Tutankhaten are also candidates, and there is an outside chance that the blinker was already old when it was brought to Amarna. It could not, however, be much older than the reign of Akhenaten's father because, while the horse and chariot had been introduced to Egypt at the start of the Eighteenth Dynasty, blinkers are first seen in the art decorating the Theban tomb of the royal scribe and overseer of the granaries, Khaemhat, which dates to the reign of Amenhotep III.[4]

The horse-owning sculptor must have been extremely wealthy, or a royal favourite, or both. Egypt's monarchs traditionally rewarded their loyal followers with lavish presents and Akhenaten was no exception. Images carved on the walls of the elite Amarna tombs show him quite literally showering his loyal supporters with gold: he stands on a balcony with his family and they stand below, arms outstretched, to receive his largesse.[5] So it is entirely possible that Thutmose received his expensive equipage as a gift from his king. It is a leap of faith – but a reasonable one – to assume that he was the owner of the extensive compound, incorporating not only luxurious living quarters and a stable for horses but also a flourishing sculptor's workshop, where the blinker was found. It is not reasonable to assume – as some have done – that all the artwork discovered within this compound should be attributed to the hand of the master-sculptor, Thutmose. In ancient Egypt, as today, any sculptor whose workshop created large-scale or multiple public works is likely to have been supported by a team of assistants and apprentices.

In the Sculptor's Workshop

Where, exactly, did Thutmose live and work? Amarna was an elongated city running north to south, and sandwiched between the River Nile to the west and limestone cliffs to the east. Its official buildings were linked by a wide processional way – today designated the Royal Road – which ran parallel to the river.[6] Subverting the tradition that chariots were primarily weapons used in fighting and hunting, the royal family used this road to display themselves to their people.

The Central City, the religious and administrative heart of Amarna, was a carefully planned zone which included the Great and the Small Aten Temple precincts, the ceremonial complex known as the Great Palace, the police and army barracks, and a warren of offices where the civil servants ran Akhenaten's extensive empire. Thutmose lived approximately a kilometre to the south of the centre, in an upmarket neighbourhood known today as the Main City. Here some of Amarna's most influential citizens occupied extensive villas, which were built alongside more humble housing and workshops producing luxury goods. To the south of the Main City lay the Southern Suburb; to the north of the Central City lay the Northern Suburb, a less prestigious area where bureaucrats lived alongside carpenters, and where fishermen and merchants – their houses identified by their extensive storage facilities – lived within easy reach of the quay. Further north still lay the North City, which included the North Riverside Palace; the private home of Akhenaten and his family.

Thutmose's extensive compound lay at the junction of East Road South, a major highway running more or less parallel to the Royal Road, and a narrower lane running at right angles to it. Behind a mud-brick wall – a physical and symbolic boundary, separating the creative world of the craftsman from the humdrum daily life of the city – lay a sizeable, square, two-storeyed villa which, it seems reasonable to assume, was Thutmose's own home.[7] A gateway opening from the lane allowed visitors to pass through a courtyard and reach the raised and canopied doorway. Beyond this, a small vestibule led to an anteroom where a doorway to the right allowed access to the plaster workshops which ran along the east side of the villa. A collection of old alabaster and obsidian artefacts, which were presumably awaiting recycling, suggests that inlays made from precious materials and maybe smaller hard stone sculptures were manufactured here.

Back in the anteroom, a doorway to the left allowed access to a columned reception hall whose plastered and painted walls were decorated with floral designs that have survived as detached fragments. Opening off the reception hall were two small interconnected rooms (Room 18 and Room 19) equipped with water jars and a table, which archaeologists have tentatively identified as pantries or larders used when entertaining guests. A door in Room 19 allowed access to the large stoneworking courtyard, and its well. Thutmose's private quarters were reached via a spacious living room, and included the master bedroom, bathroom and a non-flushing toilet. A staircase led to the now-vanished upper storey. A small, enclosed courtyard behind the villa was dominated by four large granaries capable of storing enough grain to feed not only Thutmose and his family but his workforce too, grain being, in Egypt's moneyless economy, the usual form of wage. Essentially, his granaries were Thutmose's bank, and it is not surprising that he wanted to retain complete control over access to his wealth. Four beehive-shaped mud-brick ovens provided the bread that formed an important part of the Egyptian diet.

As the business developed, a second, somewhat smaller house was added to the compound, beside the main villa. This smaller house, which had its own entrance, served as the nucleus of a cluster of relatively humble living quarters and working areas. It shared basic facilities – granaries, ovens, the stable and a well – with the main villa. It is tempting to speculate that this new accommodation was built for a member of Thutmose's immediate family, a son perhaps, who was now working alongside his father. Employment, even employment by the state, was largely hereditary, and we would expect to find Thutmose training his sons and grandsons from a young age to follow in his footsteps. He would not have trained his daughters and granddaughters; we know of no female sculptors or artists in ancient Egypt.

A wide gateway, large enough to admit the delivery of large stone blocks and the passage of a chariot, opened from East Road South into a spacious courtyard. Beyond this lay the stable that housed the chariot horses and a range of farm animals. Fragments of diorite and quartzite indicate that the heavy stone was worked in this courtyard, as close as possible to the delivery point. This would have been hot and thirsty work, and the masons would have been grateful for the large well, which was essentially a deep water-hole accessed via a winding staircase. A row of trees, planted alongside the house, would have offered welcome shade. The trees are, of course, long gone, but the pits dug for their roots remain obvious in the archaeological record. It was in one of these pits (originally identified as a rubbish pit) that Borchardt's men discovered the broken ivory blinker that allows us to name the compound's owner.

As Amarna grew, so did the demand for Thutmose's products. When the expanding business needed yet more working space the complex was extended southwards, beyond the original compound wall. This allowed the creation of new working areas, residential quarters for the workmen and apprentices, a third house and a second well. A large food container set into the floor of one of these newer units recorded the name 'Ramose' in hieratic script; this is the only non-royal name aside from Thutmose to be recovered from the workshop.[8] We know nothing more about this Ramose, who was presumably one of several workmen employed there.

Stone Kings

High-quality sculpted pieces (complete, incomplete and fragmented), sculptors' tools, stone chips, gypsum plaster artefacts and flakes of gold foil have been found throughout the extended Thutmose compound, making it clear that this was a functioning workshop. Many of these pieces have been identified as royalty, proving, as we had already suspected, that the workshop was closely linked to Akhenaten's court. A nearby but entirely separate house has yielded the remnants of a range of small-scale industries – stone working, faience manufacture, textile working and glass production – and it seems likely that goods manufactured here were supplied to the Thutmose workshop.[9] Linen, which at first sight might seem an odd requirement for a sculptor's workshop, would have been needed to clothe the finished statues. Texts tell us that temple statues were dressed each morning as part of the daily temple ritual, and this is confirmed by the discovery, in Tutankhamen's Valley of the Kings tomb, of statuettes of the king and his gods shrouded in linen cloaks.[10]

Thutmose was not Amarna's only sculptor. He lived in a city of thriving small-scale and cottage industries where, as Flinders Petrie noted during his brief excavations:

> *The sculptors' workshops proved of much interest. The most exten-*
> *sive was at the north of the palace ... Fragments of statues, trial*
> *pieces of an arm, a foot, hieroglyphs with master's corrections in*
> *black ink, and pieces of various works in stone and glaze were*
> *found here ... Another sculptor's place was found near the south*
> *end of the town, containing many stages of work, from the first*
> *practice of the beginner on the simplest sign, the neb, to more*
> *advanced studies from life.*[11]

As the early archaeologists tended to concentrate their excavations on Amarna's buildings while neglecting their courtyards, there may well be many more workshops still hidden under the Amarna sands.[12]

However, the fact that Thutmose's workshop specialised in royal statues gave him a particularly high status. Royal statues were precious items, with a value that extended far beyond the individual components of their manufacture. They were commissioned by the king and his representatives, and displayed in official contexts primarily, but not exclusively, in the Central City, which was enhanced by multiple stone images of Akhenaten and his family, many created at a larger-than-life scale. Whereas other kings had commissioned sculptures of Egypt's many gods plus the royal family, Akhenaten commissioned statues of himself and his family exclusively. The more public of these had an obvious decorative and propaganda function, but they could also serve as a focus of worship for people who were forbidden entry to the temple precincts and so denied direct access to the state god.

The statues and statue fragments recovered from the Thutmose workshop do not exhibit the huge scale of the pieces that once decorated the Great Palace and the Great Temple, but this is not unexpected. Thutmose did not run a shop and did not need to keep stock; he worked to order and his completed statues were despatched straight to their planned display site. Indeed, his larger pieces and those made of hard stone, which is as heavy as it is durable, are unlikely ever to have visited his workshop. In order to avoid transporting unnecessary weight, they would have been roughed out in the quarry then completed *in situ* in the Central City. As the sources of hard stone were situated a considerable distance from Amarna – with granite and granodiorite being quarried at the southern border town of Aswan, and quartzite being quarried either in the north, at Gebel Ahmar near modern Cairo, or in the south, at Gebel Tingar, near Aswan – this suggests that the quarries employed teams of specialist masons to work alongside their quarrymen and labourers. It may therefore be that, as part of his royal duties, Thutmose was regularly required to undertake the long river journey to the hard stone quarries, to liaise with their sculptors.

Unfortunately, no stone statue could withstand the fury of those who wished to eradicate all memory of the aberrant Amarna Period. The royal images were attacked and in many cases smashed to pieces – and so rendered ineffective as a means of accessing the divine – not long after Akhenaten's death. Official architecture was attacked too, with all of Akhenaten's religious buildings being dismantled and, in many cases, their stone blocks reused in other official buildings. This leaves us in the difficult situation of having an extensive artistic record of an extraordinary time in Egyptian history, which is almost entirely represented by fragments, defaced scenes and dispersed blocks.

The impressive series of colossal statues that once lined the courtyard of the Amarna Great Palace is today represented by a stark collection of empty statue bases plus thousands of red granite and quartzite fragments.[13] The statues which once adorned the colonnades and halls of the two Aten temple complexes were destroyed along with all the others, but live again on the carved walls of the Amarna elite tombs. Huya's tomb, for example, allows us a clear view of the interior of the Great Aten Temple, where we see multiple statues of Akhenaten and Nefertiti lining the porticoes or colonnades, many bearing rectangular offering tables loaded with gifts for the god.[14] A similar concentration of temple statues may be seen at Thebes, where Akhenaten built an open-air sun temple, Gempaaten ('the sun-disc is found'), shortly before his move to Amarna. This temple included a court lined with five-metre tall sandstone images of the king. These statues were destroyed when the temple was dismantled at the end of the Eighteenth Dynasty, but as the pieces were used as fill in later buildings, it has proved possible to reconstruct many of them.[15] It is a testament to the productivity of the royal workshops that, in spite of the post-Amarna attacks, we have more engravings and sculptures of Nefertiti than of any other Egyptian queen, Cleopatra VII included.

During the 1891–2 season of excavation at Amarna, Howard Carter discovered many fragments of royal statuary and stelae inside the remains of the Great Temple. As Petrie explains:

> *The site of the temple, or shrine, which was entirely excavated by Mr Carter, is marked by heaps of broken pieces of mortar and stone ... The absence of all sculptures was partly explained on searching the heap which lay just outside the temenos wall, on the south of the temple. Here were found portions of seventeen limestone statues of the king and queen, probably those which are represented in porticoes in the drawing of the temple ... Beside these*

lifesized statues in the temple, there were also colossal standing statues of Akhenaten, in soft limestone, of which an ear, a toe, and a piece of the chest were found. The attitude seems to have been with crossed arms holding the crook and flail, but whether standing (like an Osirian figure or ushabti) or seated (like his statue in the Louvre) is not determined.[16]

The statues and associated fragments entered the private collection of Lord Amherst, the sponsor of Petrie's Amarna expedition. The collection of fragments was subsequently sold by auction and, as a result, many are now in the collection of the Metropolitan Museum, New York. Others, as Petrie later recorded, were simply thrown away:

The torsos and fragments of the queen's face were – after Lord Amherst's death – sold for hundreds of pounds at Sotheby's, while the boxes full of flakes which should have completed them were thrown away as stone waste. Thus perished the chance of reconstructing the priceless figures of that age.[17]

A more substantial statue fragment – a female lower torso wearing a pleated robe tied with a red sash, which almost certainly represents Nefertiti – was recently discovered in the rubble used to raise the ground level during the second phase of building at the Great Temple during, or shortly after, Akhenaten's regnal year 12. The limestone used to create this statue includes significant amounts of microscopic silica (quartz), and this has allowed it to be traced to a siliceous crystalline limestone quarry situated near to Amarna's well-known Hatnub alabaster quarry. The limestone quarry has yielded cut blocks and statue roughouts that confirm that a lot of preliminary work was done in the quarry, before the heavy stone was transported to the city.[18]

The Great and Small Aten Temples were not the only official places of worship. Amarna was riddled with shrines, chapels and 'sunshade temples' provided for the private worship of the royal women. These are not always easy for us to identify or understand. During Pendlebury's 1936/7 Amarna excavation season, for example, a curious building was discovered in the border between the Central City and the Main City, on East Street South.[19] Although built of mud-brick and situated in a predominantly residential area, this was not a conventional house; its open forecourt and two columned halls suggest that it may have been a private chapel. The building yielded statue components, including a faience king's crown, twin wooden plumes that probably formed part of a (queen's?) crown, and a wooden (human) arm. A fragmented wooden shrine, which originally stood on a podium in the central room, was decorated with a painted scene which has been reconstructed to show Akhenaten smiting a group of enemies who grovel before him. Comparison with more conventional temple shrines suggests that the shrine doors (known as the 'doors of heaven') would have been opened to reveal the cult statue and allow worship and the performance of ritual. This statue is, of course, missing, but the reconstructed inscription identifies it as the 'great statue which the king caused to have made'. As the wooden shrine was found in scattered fragments, it is possible that there were originally two shrines each holding a statue, one for Akhenaten and one for Nefertiti.

The 'smiting scene' – a scene showing the king raising his arm to despatch one or more cringing enemies – was a favourite two-dimensional motif throughout the Eighteenth Dynasty. In stark contradiction of the popular modern perception of Akhenaten as a pacifist, we can see both Akhenaten and Nefertiti killing Egypt's enemies in scenes carved at both Amarna and Karnak. Although it is generally assumed that this is a symbolic image, it may be that we are witnessing an actual ritual. Remote killing – the idea that a host of foreign enemies might be vanquished by Egyptian temple rituals – was an accepted means of defeating foes, and the effect would presumably have been magnified had the ritual involved the despatch of an actual token enemy. Real or not, the image of the king as a victorious warrior killing representative enemies of Egypt is an obvious illustration of *maat* in action: pharaoh fulfilling his duty to subdue the chaos, represented by the foreigners, which constantly threatens the status quo within Egypt. The image of the queen smiting female prisoners in exactly the same way is, as far as we know, an innovation during Akhenaten's reign.[20]

Statues may have been commissioned as part of the royal burial equipment but, as the Amarna royal tomb was emptied in antiquity and stripped again by modern looters, our only guide as to what it might have contained comes once again from Tutankhamen's tomb, which was sealed no more than fifteen years after Akhenaten's death. As a devotee of Amen, Tutankhamen must have had afterlife expectations very different from those of his predecessor, and we cannot assume that the two kings were interred with the same range of grave goods. Nevertheless, it is worth noting that Tutankhamen was buried with a large number of three-dimensional images of himself. These range from a pair of life-sized 'guardian statues' which protected the entrance to the Burial Chamber, to a series of small-scale gilded wooden statuettes recovered from the Treasury.[21] It seems that later Eighteenth Dynasty kings might, indeed, be buried with multiple images of themselves, but that these images were likely to be created from wood rather than stone. This makes sense. Wood was never seen as a cheap option in Egypt, a land lacking tall trees. A wooden figure was a prized item which would serve exactly the same function within the tomb as a statue made from stone. True, wood was a more ephemeral material, but it was lighter and therefore easier to work and transport than stone and, once in place, the wooden statue would be protected by the stone tomb, which was itself designed to last until the end of time. Stone, being more durable than wood, was connected with ideas of permanence and longevity, and this made it a highly suitable medium for public or outdoor art.

We would have expected to find statues in Akhenaten's mortuary temple; the temple which represented the public aspect of the king's funerary provision where, under a more orthodox regime, offerings would be made on a daily basis to the dead king. However, Akhenaten's mortuary temple is missing, and we are left to wonder if the Small Aten Temple, which was aligned towards the royal tomb, fulfilled this function. His father's mortuary temple, once the largest royal temple in dynastic Egypt, is missing too. However, in this case we know precisely where it stood as the site, at Kom el-Hetan on the west bank of the Nile at Thebes, is still guarded by a pair huge quartzite seated kings, known today as the Colossi of Memnon. We know what the temple looked like, too:

> *A monument of eternity and everlastingness, of fine sandstone worked with gold throughout … It is enriched with statues of the lord [Amenhotep III], of granite, quartzite and of all kinds of precious stones, worked in enduring workmanship. Their height rises to heaven.*[22]

The temple was graced with numerous hard stone images of Amenhotep III, family groups of the more important state gods, and a zoo of sacred animal statues including sphinxes, rams and jackals. Most remarkable of all were the multiple granodiorite statues of the fierce lioness goddess Sekhmet.[23] Approximately 600 of these statues have been recovered, and it is assumed that originally there were 730 of them, one seated and one standing for each day of the year. At first glance, the Sekhmets appear identical. Closer inspection, however, reveals minor differences in execution which seem to reflect the varying skills of the team of sculptors engaged in their production. These differences would have been less obvious if the Sekhmets were painted or gilded, and they certainly would not have affected the effectiveness of the statues which, we assume, were intended to protect the ageing king against illness throughout the entire year.

Unlike his father, Akhenaten had no use for stone gods or goddesses. His god had started life as a falcon-headed deity, but from regnal year 4 onwards had become a faceless, bodiless disc which hung in the sky emitting long, thin rays ending in tiny human hands. These hands were important, as they allowed the Aten to interact with the royal family just as the traditional gods had previously interacted with kings and queens, by supporting their crowns, for example, or holding the *ankh*, symbol of life, above their heads.[24] Although this tableau could be depicted quite satisfactorily in two-dimensional art, it was simply impossible in 3D. This was not a problem, however, as the Aten temples could dispense with cult statues altogether. Akhenaten's god could be accessed directly, through the open temple roof. The *benben* – a solar cult object linked to the cult of the sun god Re of Heliopolis since the start of the dynastic age – offered an alternative focus for worship. Over the centuries the *benben* had varied in appearance from temple to temple; it might be a cone- or pyramid-shaped structure, an obelisk, a boulder or even a meteorite. The Amarna *benben* has not survived, but images in the elite tombs suggest that it was a large, round-topped stela which stood on a raised platform next to a large statue of a seated Akhenaten.[25]

We might quite reasonably deduce that the Aten had no need for temples; that the sun could simply be worshipped in an unstructured way by anyone who stepped outdoors and looked up at the sky. But Atenism was not a democratic religion, and the common people were not expected or even encouraged to worship the state god. This was the privilege of the elite, with the temples allowing the priests and the royal family to control access to the god and his valuable resources. It was here, hidden from public view, that the Aten – a greedy god – accepted the generous offerings of food, drink and flowers that he craved. To accommodate his needs, the Great Temple was provided with almost a thousand mud-brick offering tables.

Prominent citizens who could not access the temple were expected to worship the Aten using the royal family as intermediaries. For this purpose, their homes were furnished with statues of the king and queen, or carved stone stelae depicting the royal family going about their daily business beneath the Aten's rays. These served both as an aid to official worship and as a very obvious means of demonstrating loyalty to the regime.

The End of an Era

Akhenaten died in his regnal year 17 and was buried, as he had wished, in the still incomplete royal tomb. Initially, Amarna life continued as it always had done. A wine jar fragment recovered from Thutmose's villa bears an inscription dating the wine to 'year 1' of an anonymous king.[26] A broken blue faience ring discovered in the Thutmose compound takes the form of a cartouche inscribed with the name Nebkheperure: the throne name of Tutankhamen.[27] Combined, these two pieces of evidence suggest that the workshop continued under the new regime. But then, in Tutankhamen's regnal year 3 or year 4, came the decision to reverse the Amarna experiment. The traditional gods were to be reinstated and the court was to relocate. The southern city of Thebes would be restored to its position as Egypt's religious capital, while the northern city of Memphis would once again be Egypt's administrative hub. A large stela erected in the Karnak Temple at Thebes, and dedicated to the newly restored Amen, explains Tutankhamen's pious desire to placate the old regime:

> *Now when His Majesty [Tutankhamen] arose as king, the temples of the gods and goddesses, beginning from Elephantine to the marshes of the Delta, had fallen into neglect, their shrines had fallen into desolation and become tracts overgrown with weeds, their sanctuaries were as if they had never been, their halls were a trodden path. The land was in confusion, the gods forsook this land ... After some days had passed, [His Majesty appeared] on the throne of his father; he ruled the countries of Horus, the Black Land and the Red Land were under his dominion, and every land was in obeisance to his might ... Then His Majesty took counsel with his heart, searching out every excellent occasion, seeking what was beneficial to his father Amen.*[28]

We cannot take this statement literally. Tutankhamen's body, discovered lying undisturbed in his sealed sarcophagus, shows that he was approximately eighteen years old when he died, while wine-jar dates from his tomb suggest that he reigned for approximately ten years. Tutankhamen was therefore a child of maybe eight years when he came to the throne. He would have been far too young to make such an important decision and, indeed, having been born at Amarna and raised in the cult of the Aten, he would probably have been unaware that such a decision could be made. It is doubtful that he knew much, if anything, about Amen of Thebes, the god who was now his 'father'. This was a decision made by advisors who could remember the old ways, who felt no personal devotion to the Aten, and who found Amarna an inconvenient city from which to govern an empire. It was time to go home.

A Negative Collection

Amarna had been built to service Akhenaten and his god. Without Tutankhamen's support, it was unviable. Slowly but surely the city population dwindled until Amarna was empty. One of the last houses to be occupied in the North Suburb was owned by a man named Hatiay whose name and titles, helpfully carved on a door lintel, tell us that he was the 'overseer of works, confidente of the Lord of the Two Lands'.[29] While the houses all around show evidence of looting, Hatiay's house retains a relatively large amount of stone masonry suggesting that he remained at Amarna long after his neighbours had departed. Given his impressive title, it may even be that he was charged with overseeing the official evacuation of the city, and the reuse of many of its stone elements.

Thutmose – entirely dependent on royal patronage for his livelihood – had little choice but to follow his new king. Packing his goods and chattels, and leaving the items that he no longer needed, he sailed away from Amarna. His abandoned property constitutes what archaeologists term a 'negative collection': a collection of things that Thutmose did not want, things that he could not move, and things that he had lost or forgotten. In this respect his excavated workshop differs from Pompeii or the *Titanic*, where a sudden, unanticipated disaster preserved an almost complete snapshot of daily life (albeit, in the case of the *Titanic*, an atypical daily life), and differs again from Tutankhamen's tomb, which was packed with goods deliberately selected for burial alongside the king.

In Thutmose's private villa the pantries (Rooms 18 and 19) were converted into a storage area, with the external door leading to the courtyard bricked up. Here, on 6 and 7 December 1912, Borchardt's team discovered a jumble of more than fifty artefacts made from limestone, quartzite and gypsum plaster, including the bust of Nefertiti which he believed had fallen off a shelf, although the lack of damage to the extremities makes this seem unlikely. The collection also included a similarly styled but deliberately damaged painted bust of Akhenaten, a collection of plaster 'portrait' heads and several unfinished stone sculptures, some still covered in the black ink lines used to guide the craftsmen.[30] There were at least three other Nefertitis: an unfinished and fragmented limestone statue, a plaster model and an unfinished limestone head wearing traces of a crown.[31] Amongst all these artefacts the Nefertiti bust stands out as being substantially intact and complete. It is not, however, the most curious find.

During the course of his own Amarna excavations Petrie had discovered a plaster cast or mask 'rough on the back, and without any name or mark' which he identified as the death mask of Akhenaten:

That this is a death-mask and not modelled by hand, is shewn by the delicacy of the curves of the bone, by the flattening of the ear in casting, by the absence of modelled detail in the lips, and by the similar absence of detail in the eye, reinforced, however, by added lines done by a graving-tool to make it clearer. In all these points it is clearly not made by hand. The fillet on the head was to keep back the hair in casting.[32]

The identification was later supported by the sculptor Alfred Gilbert, creator of the 'Eros' figure on the Shaftesbury Memorial Fountain at London's Piccadilly Circus. Petrie's death mask developed an instant fame which abated only when Borchardt's men discovered twenty-three similar but better made gypsum plaster faces and heads in Thutmose's pantry. Four of these pieces were sculpted heads, nineteen were faces with or without ears, and there were also four isolated body parts: an ear, a mouth and two feet. Although they were initially described as being 'some ... from the living, others from the dead model; others, again, are apparently casts of statue-faces', this is unlikely as death masks cast from the face of the deceased are unknown in ancient Egypt.[33]

Borchardt believed that, while some of the masks had been cast from stone statues, others had been cast from living individuals, and he catalogued them accordingly. Art historian Günther Roeder then suggested that they might be casts taken from clay models as part of the sculpting process; this also seems unlikely, as there is no other evidence to suggest that Egypt's sculptors worked with clay models.[34] Recently, it has been accepted that they are probably casts taken from finished statues, created, perhaps, to guide the royal artists in their work and serve as a reference for future works. The fact that some of the masks have hollow eyes and eyebrows indicates that they were cast before the precious inlays were added to the statues. As they would have been both cheap to produce and easy to transport, identical plaster masks might have been circulated to workshops throughout the empire, ensuring that the royal image remained constant wherever it might appear. Thutmose's pantry may, therefore, have housed his reference library. We can deduce that the masks were made on the premises, as quantities of gypsum plaster were discovered in the courtyards and in the workrooms running alongside the villa.

As none of the plaster masks is labelled, Egyptologists have struggled to attribute them to specific individuals. The preliminary sorting is easy; it is obvious that some of the original statues were equipped with wigs while others – the royals – had crowns. On this basis we can be confident that the collection includes nine royals (four heads and five faces). While the royal masks tend to be slightly smaller than life-sized and to display idealised features, the non-royals are life-sized and appear to be true, and not always flattering, representations of real people. Dietrich Wildung, who has described them as 'old, haggard and ugly', has suggested that their extreme realism is a sign that they are not members of the elite, who would have been represented as stereotypically perfect, but members of the lower classes: 'stable boys and workers, whose miserable living conditions have been testified to in a horrifying manner by the graves uncovered at the edge of the desert in recent years'.[35] This seems a little harsh: the non-royal faces, while not idealised, are by no means as repulsive as Wildung suggests. It may be that these are models for the statues which would have been added to the elite tombs, had any of them been finished before Amarna was abandoned.

Two of the plaster faces have been identified, on the basis of their hairstyle and large, round earrings or ear plugs, as Kiya, a secondary queen of Akhenaten. The two masks are not identical but they are similar enough to suggest that they represent the same person, and neither resembles either Nefertiti or her daughters. We have no confirmed portrait of Kiya in the round, but several 2D images allow us to recognise her oval, slightly smiling face, her firm chin and her inevitable round earrings or ear plugs. Under normal circumstances, secondary or harem queens remained in the background, and we known little about them. But Kiya was uniquely prominent at Amarna, where she was allowed to play a part in the rituals of Aten worship.

Postscript: Thutmose after Amarna

Until relatively recently, Thutmose's story ended here. Then, on 24 November 1996, a French mission led by Egyptologist Alain Zivie, excavating in the Sakkara necropolis, discovered an insignificant, thoroughly looted private tomb belonging to a late Eighteenth Dynasty artist named Thutmose. Thutmose's title, proudly displayed on the tomb wall, identifies him as the chief of the *sesh ked* – the chief of painters or chief of draughtsmen – in the *set maat*, or Place of Truth.[36]

The Sakkara necropolis is part of the ancient and extensive cemetery associated with the equally ancient royal city and administrative centre of Memphis. Alongside some of Egypt's earliest pyramids, it houses the tombs of many of Egypt's most successful bureaucrats, officials and court favourites, including individuals who first came to prominence at Amarna. Maya, Tutankhamen's wet nurse, built an impressive tomb here, and this second Thutmose built his tomb near to hers. Long after Maya's and Thutmose's tombs were sealed, the area around their tombs was remodelled for the burial of mummified cats, sacred to the goddess Bastet and, because of this, this area is known as the Bubasteion.

The 'Place of Truth' is less easy for us to pinpoint. There is an automatic assumption that this must be a reference to the Valley of the Kings, because the specialist workers who built the royal tombs, and who lived in the state-owned village of Deir el-Medina, often referred to themselves as the 'servants in the Place of Truth'. During the Amarna Period there was no significant work in the Valley. Deir el-Medina was abandoned, and it seems that the workforce was moved wholesale to Amarna. Here they occupied a brand-new state-owned workmen's village, and laboured to create the rock-cut tombs in the nearby cliffs. With the decision to close Amarna, they were returned to Deir el-Medina, and picked up their former lives.

However, Egypt recognised more than one 'Place of Truth'. The term could be used to designate any place connected in general with sacred or holy ground and, more specifically, with tombs, cemeteries and the west (the west bank being the usual location of Egypt's cemeteries).[37] It is therefore possible that Thutmose's Place of Truth was located at Amarna, and that it is actually a reference to the royal and elite tombs in the Amarna cliffs. If we visit Tutu's rock-cut tomb, we can read his prayer to the Aten, which includes a hope for a proper burial in the Amarna 'Place of Truth':

It is with arms worshipping you and eyes beholding you without cease that I have come to you – for you are the life-giving (?) breeze [that sustains the king (or similar). May he grant] a good burial in the mountains of Akhet-Aten, the Place of Truth. For the ka of the chamberlain Tutu, justified.[38]

One of a row of tombs cut into a south-facing cliff face, Thutmose's Sakkara tomb is both simple and, in comparison to the tombs around it, very small. A now-vanished wooden door would once have kept the sand out of his eternal home. Today a well-cut but undecorated facade opens directly into a short corridor leading into a chapel with one stone pillar; the left (west) wall of the chapel incorporates an alcove housing the shaft which allows access to the subterranean burial chamber. Unlike the private subterranean burial chamber, this chapel was a public room, designed to attract visitors who might be persuaded to leave an offering which would benefit the soul of the deceased. To encourage this, the walls were decorated with a colourful mixture of sunken relief, paintings and brief texts featuring the deceased and his family. Thutmose is not the only chief of workmen in the Place of Truth to appear on these walls; in addition to his father, Amenemwia, we can see the artist Kenana and his family. It seems that Thutmose and Kenana are colleagues; the fact that they share a tomb suggests that they are also related, maybe as brothers-in-law. Thutmose is, however, the dominant tomb occupant, and the more important scenes belong to him. Zivie believes that it was Thutmose himself who created the intimate scenes of his own family. This was not without precedent; the workmen of Deir el-Medina also used their skills, honed on the royal tombs, to create their own, beautifully decorated family tombs.

The walls to the left of the entrance to the burial chamber display what Zivie has designated a 'triptych': three linked scenes presented in chronological order and designed to be read as a history, although the corner created by the niche makes it impossible to see all three at the same time. The first of these scenes introduces us to Amenemwia, an artist whose name – literally 'Amen is in the boat' – suggests that he may have been born at Thebes. Amenemwia's wife, Mutemweskhet – literally 'Mut [the goddess wife of Amen] is in the broad hall' – has a similarly Theban name. The fact that Amenemwia and Mutemweskhet are depicted on the walls of their son's tomb does not mean that they were buried with him, and it is tempting to speculate that they were buried at Thebes. Next we meet Thutmose, who is dressed in an unremarkable white linen kilt, wig and broad bead collar, and who carries a stylised painter's palette inscribed with the name of Amenhotep III. Thutmose is supported by his wife Iniy, and we see their children Itiu, Djedet and Mutemweskhet known as Tuy. Finally, we see a unique double coffin from which the full faces of Thutmose and Iniy look directly at the tomb visitor. The accompanying text tells us that this curiosity was designed by Thutmose himself. Whether or not the couple were eventually interred in one coffin is not clear – this could pose some practical difficulties – but the effect is unsettling. Standing beside the coffin, Thutmose's children offer to their deceased parents. Elsewhere in the tomb, an unfinished scene shows Thutmose and Amenemwia standing before the god of the afterlife, Osiris. Again, Thutmose carries the painter's palette which defines his role in society.

Thutmose's inscribed palette links him directly to Amenhotep III, but his tomb also includes references to the Aten, and his father's name is in places 'corrected' with the 'Amen' element being replaced by the more politically acceptable 'Re'. This suggests that Thutmose was one of a family of later Eighteenth Dynasty artists who worked on royal projects throughout the Amarna Period and beyond. Could the Sakkara Thutmose be the Amarna Thutmose? The dates certainly fit, the name is the same, and the title is similar, if not identical. The Amarna Thutmose ran a sculptor's workshop, while the Sakkara Thutmose wished to be remembered as a painter, but we know that the Amarna workshop produced beautifully painted works, and it is entirely possible that Thutmose was a painter rather than a sculptor. This may be a coincidence – the name Thutmose was certainly not an uncommon one – but it may be that Zivie's discovery allows us to place our Thutmose in a wider, pre- and post-Amarna context. This allows us to end our chapter with an indulgent paragraph of unabashed speculation:

Thutmose son of Amenemwia was born into a family of highly respected sculptors, carvers and painters. The family lived and worked in Thebes, where they ran a successful workshop engaged on royal and occasional private projects connected with the west bank tombs and temples. Trained by his father, Thutmose became an accomplished craftsman then, following his father's death, he took control of the family business. When the court moved to Amarna, he sensed a good business opportunity and moved too, setting up a new workshop to meet the almost insatiable demand for royal statuary. Married to Iniy, sister of his fellow-sculptor Kenana, he raised a family who lived and worked alongside him. While Akhenaten ruled, Thutmose was a privileged royal favourite. When the Amarna experiment ended Thutmose and his family moved to Memphis, where he continued to work for the state and the temples while creating his own family tomb. Here, eventually, he was buried with his wife and his brother-in-law, in a tomb whose walls he himself had decorated.

2

CHIEF OF WORKS

There really is no such thing as Art. There are only artists.[1]

E. H. Gombrich (1950)

The European Renaissance introduced the West to the idea of the artist as an individual. Our sculptors and painters are respected because they have the mysterious, God-given ability to create 'Art': a word that, while often spoken in hushed tones, somehow manages to convey a capital 'A'. They are independent beings, free to design and sell their work as they see fit, and, although their work may be commissioned by patrons who make explicit demands on their skills, that work remains a part of the artist's catalogue.[2]

Under totalitarian regimes, where art is considered a necessary part of the official propaganda machine, there is likely to be far less freedom of expression. Nevertheless, personal skill may still be appreciated, and an individual artist may be celebrated for his or her works. Dynastic Egypt may be classed as a totalitarian regime. Here, the most talented sculptors were employed by kings and temples.

They were expected to work to predetermined rules, and their completed works would be placed in specific locations to fulfil particular functions. It is this official art, primarily that carved in stone to ornament stone buildings, that has survived in the archaeological record and which, stripped from its original context and purpose, now decorates the sculpture halls of our Western museums and galleries. It does not take a great deal of imagination to see these galleries as the modern equivalent of the ancient palaces and temples they so often resemble, and the visitors who fill those galleries as a self-selecting elite who come to admire if not to worship. Thus, it can be argued that, 2,000 years after the end of the dynastic age, Egyptian sculpture has simply transferred from one sacred context to another.[3]

This very practical approach to the creating of official art explains why, although many royal statues were inscribed, none of the inscriptions included the name of the sculptor. Skill was appreciated, sought out and rewarded, but individuality was not a desirable attribute in a royal artist, and the name of the sculptor did not add the premium that it might in today's commercial art world. As we saw when we considered Amenhotep's 730 near-matching Sekhmet statues, a royal or divine statue would be equally effective, and so equally valuable, whether it was made by an apprentice, a master craftsmen or, as seems most likely, a team of specialist workers and trainees. The only important name was the name of the subject or the patron who commissioned the work; in the case of royal statues, these were usually one and the same.

The Egyptians had no word corresponding to our word 'art', although there was a word, *hemet*, used to denote skill or craft, and from this word came the noun *hemuw*, meaning 'expert' or 'craftsman'. At Memphis, the high priest of Ptah bore the simple title *wer kherep hemut*, or 'master craftsman'. This lack of a specific word, combined with the fact that all official Egyptian art had a function beyond the aesthetic, has led some Egyptologists to make the deliberately provocative statement that there is 'no such thing as "Egyptian art"',[4] suggesting that Thutmose and his colleagues should perhaps be reclassified as artisans or craftsmen, as presumably should all European pre-Renaissance sculptors and painters, and many other artists from many other cultures too. This makes an interesting semantic argument, but it is unlikely that Thutmose would care overmuch how he was categorised by theorists living in a very different world from his own. He did the work that was required of him and he and his patrons understood its true value. 'Art' is in any case notoriously incapable of a rigid definition as its meaning varies both from community to community and within the same community through time, while the border between arts and crafts is always a fluid one. We are comfortable with the idea that sculpture and painting can be classified as art, or even 'fine art'. But are we to classify Egypt's beautiful jewellery, exquisitely embroidered robes and colourful decorated tiles as art, or craft? And, more importantly, how did their creators classify them?

The image of Thutmose the solitary genius, working alone in his studio to carve an image of his beautiful queen, is a seductive one. However, the evidence from his workshop – an industrial unit rather than a studio – shows that it is entirely wrong. Thutmose, 'chief of works', was an accomplished administrator who owned, or at least managed, a thriving business. He was an important link in a complex and expensive chain of transactions that started with stone blocks being cut in the quarry and ended with a finished product being delivered to the Main City. Did he also sculpt? Did he add a few final touches to the work done by his apprentices? Or did he simply manage the workshop? This is not clear, but we can perhaps get a better sense of Thutmose's duties if we look at the evidence provided by his fellow Amarna sculptor Iuty, 'chief sculptor of the King's Great Wife Tiy'.

Iuty is featured with an unexpected prominence on the wall of

The Overseer of Sculptors, Iuty, completing a statue of Princess Baketaten in his workshop. After Davies 1905, vol. III, Plate XVIII

Huya's Amarna tomb.[5] Huya is Iuty's boss, and so we are left with the intriguing possibility that Iuty himself created this scene; this would certainly explain why he is so clearly labelled. By immortalising himself in Huya's robust tomb, Iuty would have accrued many of the benefits of the tomb owner. His labelled image might even have been his personal route to a satisfactory afterlife. We see Iuty as he sits on a low stool in a columned hall, dressed in a pleated kilt and wig. He is bending forward to put the finishing touches to the face of a statue of Princess Baketaten, Tiy's youngest daughter. In his left hand Iuty holds an artist's palette, in his right a paintbrush. It is not clear whether the statue that he is working on is wooden or stone. Behind the statue stands a smaller – and therefore less important – anonymous workman, who bows slightly as he watches Iuty at work. The figure who once stood behind Iuty is now missing, but two small-scale workmen can be seen sitting on stools; one is carving a wooden chair leg and the other is using a chisel to work on what seems to be a small stone head. In a distant part of the room other seated craftsmen work on a wooden box and stone vessels.

What, exactly, is Iuty doing? Here we must turn to the Egyptian language for guidance. The Egyptians employed two words which we routinely translate as 'sculptor'; as far as we can tell, these words were used interchangeably but, as we are chronologically and culturally far removed from ancient Egypt, it may be that we are failing to pick up on subtle differences in meaning. The first word, *gnwt*, carried no additional connotation. The second word, *s'ankh*, is the word used on Thutmose's horse blinker; it translates as 'the one who makes alive'. This reflects a crucial aspect of the Egyptian sculptor's role. Sculptors, like gods, were creators. By releasing a shape from an amorphous stone block, they created a latent form capable of life. Performance of the correct rituals could then convert that form into a functioning entity which could, if necessary, serve as a substitute body capable of housing the soul of its subject. Akhenaten's many statues were not only decorative but also an insurance policy. If his planned afterlife failed his stone bodies might, in extremis, serve as a home for his *ka*, or soul. Under a more orthodox regime, statues might also house the gods.

Iuty is painting Baketaten's face. His touching of the eyes, ears, nose and mouth with his brush is reminiscent of the 'opening-of-the-mouth ceremony'; a ritual said to have been devised by the creator god Ptah to convert mummies, statues and two-dimensional images into latent beings with a potential for life. By the Eighteenth Dynasty this was one of the most important parts of the funerary ritual, invariably performed at the entrance to the tomb. The mummy was propped upright as the *sem*-priest touched it with a series of sacred objects including a flint knife similar to that used to cut the umbilical cord at birth, an adze and the leg of an ox. Meanwhile, the lector-priest recited the spells that would reanimate the mummy, making it ready for the life to come. Is the application of the final layer of paint in the sculptor's workshop, or perhaps in the temple, the way that a *s'ankh* added the potential for life to an already complete stone sculpture?

We can learn more about the religious aspect of the sculptor's role by examining a slightly later piece; an inscribed stela belonging to the late Eighteenth or early Nineteenth Dynasty, 'chief sculptor of the Lord of the Two Lands, Hatiay, son of the chief sculptor Ya'.[6] Whether this Hatiay and the overseer of works Hatiay, whom we met as he supervised the evacuation of Amarna, are the same man is not clear, but they would have been contemporaries, and their titles are not mutually exclusive. Chief sculptor Hatiay modestly, and almost certainly misleadingly, given that he admits to being the son of a chief sculptor, tells us that he came from a humble background, yet he was allowed privileged access to the king, whom he saw 'in his form of Re in the seclusion of his palace'. Furthermore:

> *He [the king] appointed me to direct the works when I was only a youngster, for he had found that I was someone he could count on. I was initiated into the House of Gold in order to fashion the cult statues and the sacred images of all the gods, without any of them being hidden from me. I was a master of secrets.*[7]

Here we have a sculptor who has not been trained as a priest, yet who is allowed to enter the 'House of Gold', a restricted workshop within the temple where statues were created. Did Hatiay bring life to the temple statues in the House of Gold? How did he do this? Using spells, or paint, or both? As we have already seen, at Amarna the 'cult statues and sacred images of all the gods' that would be found in most state temples were replaced by multiple images of the king and his family. Did the age-old rituals continue to be performed on the Amarna royal statues, perhaps by Thutmose himself?

Their ability to both create and animate linked Hatiay, Iuty, Thutmose and all of Egypt's sculptors to Ptah, patron deity of all masons, builders and sculptors. Ptah's theology tell us that he had the ability to create life using his heart; as the heart was believed to be the centre of thought, this means that he planned and crafted his creations just as Thutmose may have planned his sculptures. First Ptah created the gods, then he created their shrines. Then: 'He made their bodies according to their wishes. Thus the gods entered into their bodies, of every wood, every stone, every clay ... Thus were gathered to him all the gods and their souls.'[8]

Ptah, of course, like Osiris, belonged to the traditional pantheon and so was not openly celebrated at Amarna. Nevertheless, a direct connection with the divine might explain Thutmose's ownership of a chariot. The artist who had the power to release a royal image from a block of stone was likely to enjoy an unusually close bond with his patron, and might well be the recipient of generous gifts.

Men and Bak

This link to the divine provides a second good reason why Egypt's royal sculptors never signed their work. To add a non-royal name to a royal sculpture would have forged a permanent and unacceptable bond between the sculptor, his royal subject and his creation. As names, like images, could serve as a home for the soul, the addition of his name might have allowed the sculptor to share a part of the royal afterlife. That would have been unthinkable. We know of just one example where a commoner dared to add his name to a royal creation. Earlier in the Eighteenth Dynasty, the courtier Senenmut had carved over sixty small representations of himself within King Hatshepsut's Deir el-Bahri mortuary temple. These images were added to walls that would usually be covered by the open doors of shrines and statue niches, so that they would have been completely hidden during the performance of the temple rituals. However, it is hard to imagine that such a blatant breach of etiquette would have gone unnoticed and unreported, and while it is possible that Hatshepsut approved of her favourite's attempts to associate himself with her cult for all eternity, it is equally possible that this bold move contributed towards his downfall.[9] Away from the court the situation was different, and the less exalted craftsmen who created statuettes and carved stelae to sell to their non-royal neighbours saw nothing wrong in adding their own name to the inscription so that they might benefit from any blessing accruing to the owner.

It is not surprising that we know few of Akhenaten's sculptors by name. Thutmose is known because of an accidentally preserved inscription on a horse blinker. Iuty is known because he features in the Amarna tomb of Huya. Hatiay is known because he inscribed his autobiography on a stela. A second stela – this time a form of elite graffiti rather than an authorised memorial – carved in a granite quarry in the southern border-town of Aswan, introduces us to two more:

Giving adoration to the Lord of the Two Lands and kissing the ground to Waenre [Akhenaten] by the overseer of works projects in the Red Mountain, a disciple whom his majesty [Akhenaten] himself instructed, chief of sculptors in the big and important monuments of the king in the House of Aten, in Akhet-Aten, Bak, the son of the chief of sculptors Men, and born of the housewife Ry of Heliopolis.[10]

Here we have a father and son, Men and Bak, who worked for a father and son, Amenhotep III and Akhenaten. The carved scene shows the two sculptors standing before their respective kings. On the right Men stands, arms raised, before a table laden with 'every good and pure thing, consisting of bread, beer, long-horned oxen [short horned cattle], fowl, and all sorts of fine vegetables'. He is offering this feast to a huge seated statue of Amenhotep III and, in so doing, raises the possibility that he was personally involved in the production of the colossi that sat outside Amenhotep's mortuary temple. Amenhotep's statue appears entirely conventional in design, and the stone king is both impassive and impressive.

Men must have been a busy man. Amenhotep's unusually long and phenomenally wealthy reign allowed him to commission art and architecture on an almost unimaginable scale, and the numbers are startling. We have already considered his 730 Sekhmet statues. We must add to these many hundreds of monumental stone statues showing Amenhotep as a king or a god, with more than forty-five of these being built at a colossal – above life-sized – scale. We have no idea how many stone statues have been lost, destroyed or renamed, and no idea how many statues were created from the less durable wood or metal, but the total number of statues is likely to be considerably above a thousand. As a result, we have more life-sized and above life-sized statues of Amenhotep than of any other pharaoh.

To the left of their shared stela, Bak also stands, arms raised, before a loaded offering table. Opposite him stands his king, Akhenaten, his arms lifted in praise of the Aten, who shines down on the king (but not on the sculptor) from above. Akhenaten's image has been vandalised, but we can see that, in contrast to his father, he does not present the appearance of a conventional, or even an impressive king. His body is softer and more feminine than Amenhotep's, with heavy thighs and a rounded stomach. In the accompanying inscription, Bak tells us that he not only worked for Akhenaten but also was taught by him.

A quartzite naos, or sculpted stela, offers a second view of Bak.[11]

Here he stands next to his wife, Tahere, with both facing forward to look straight at the viewer. Tahere embraces her husband with her left arm. She wears a long wig and a simple, tight-fitting sheath dress that outlines her body. But the eye is drawn to Bak, whose elaborately pleated garment does nothing to detract from his unusually prominent, almost pregnant-looking stomach and heavy breasts. It was not unusual for elderly men to be depicted with rolls of fat – only the very successful could afford a lifestyle that would allow them to put on weight, and such success deserved to be celebrated – but this is unusually exaggerated. Again, the accompanying text emphasises the fact that Bak was a pupil or disciple of his king. This may, of course, be simple flattery. It seems to have been impossible to overpraise any pharaoh; subtlety was simply not appreciated at the Egyptian court. Akhenaten was particularly keen to be acknowledged as a teacher or leader, and so we find even the highly experienced courtier Tutu diplomatically acknowledging his king as his mentor on his Amarna tomb wall: 'For every day he rises early to instruct me inasmuch as I execute his teaching, and no instance of any wickedness of mine can be found … the teaching of the Lord of the Two Lands.'[12]

But Bak's words may also be read as an explanation, and maybe even an apology. For Bak, who has been taught by his master-sculptor father, and who knows full well what a proper Egyptian king should look like, has started to create a very different style of art on the orders of his king.

Royal Decorum

From the very start of the dynastic age it had been accepted that the king of Egypt should be depicted with appropriate decorum. He should be the dominant human in any scene; he should be shown with a calm face and a physically perfect body; he should wear specific clothes and accessories (including crowns and head-cloths), carry a range of diagnostic regalia (including the false beard, and the crook and flail), and perform a recognised range of actions designed to emphasise his role as the upholder of *maat*; he should stand, sit or kneel.

Sometimes the king's pose would carry an immediate message. We have already encountered the 'smiting scene', a popular two-dimensional motif for exterior temple walls during the New Kingdom. More subtle was the image of the seated king which could be read as a rebus with the throne, or *set*, representing the goddess Isis (whose name literally means 'throne'), and the king representing her son Horus, the divine representative of all of Egypt's living kings. In a similar way, a standing statue with the legs close together allowed the king to mimic Osiris, the mummified god who represented all of Egypt's dead kings. That Egypt's kings used their art as a means of promoting differing versions of themselves should come as no surprise; we see a similar situation if we look at our own royalty, whose official art shows them wearing specific clothes and accessories (crowns, awards and uniforms), carrying diagnostic regalia (the orb and sceptre, for example), and performing a recognised range of actions designed to emphasise chosen aspects of their role. Today's official images tend to be films and photographs rather than paintings or sculptures, and they are therefore accurate representations of people whom most of their subjects would recognise. But a glimpse at Britain's coins, banknotes and postage stamps confirms that a royal image can be instantly recognisable without being an exact likeness.

In ancient Egypt, the conventional representation of the monarch served as a stone hieroglyph, to be read as the non gender-specific word 'king'. Such was the power of the word that the image would reinforce its own message, transforming into the fearless upholder of *maat* every king who chose to be depicted as such. Few would ever see their king and few could read his name, but the city-dwellers at least would see multiple images, which would serve as confirmation that their king was the continuation of all who had gone before. So entrenched was the belief that there was only one way to represent a king, that the female pharaoh Hatshepsut had herself depicted in formal art with the traditional (male) king's body and accessories. The intention was not to deceive anyone into thinking that she was a man. Rather, she wished to show her people and her gods that she was a proper king. Similarly, the Twentieth Dynasty king Siptah, a young man whose well-preserved mummy confirms that he had a twisted leg and foot, was depicted with two conventionally straight legs.[13] Again, the aim was not to deceive, or to hide the fact that Siptah was different, but to show that Siptah was the correct king of Egypt in every sense of the word. We don't have to look too hard to find other examples where the conventional image takes precedence over reality: elderly kings who appear eternally young; young kings who appear wise beyond their years; male kings whose buck-teeth and smallpox scars go unrecorded; a female king whose uncomfortable mixture of women's and royal clothing was surely not worn on a daily basis.[14]

The Egyptians used the word *tut*, which translates as 'likeness', or even 'perfect likeness', to describe their statues, relief sculpture and paintings.[15] This word was followed by a determinative (a sign indicating the meaning of the word) that took the form of either a statue or a mummy, reminding us that statues could substitute for mummies, with both functioning as likenesses of the subject. Following the opening-of-the-mouth ceremony, both the image and the mummy became a *tut ankh*, or a living image. So it was important that the statue was a recognisable 'likeness'; this likeness, however, did not have to be exact. It was primarily the addition of the regalia that identified the statue as a king, and the addition of the name that identified it as a particular king or, indeed, a particular mummy. The same principle applied in the non-royal art world. Craftsmen working in the private market sold off-the-peg figures that could be customised with the addition of an inscription, then donated to the temple or included amongst grave goods. Tomb artists decorated walls with painted scenes showing near-identical, ageless men and women dressed in fashionable wigs, garments and jewellery. In all cases it was the addition of the name that converted the standard image into a specific person. This system was, of course, open to abuse. An unscrupulous man might steal a temple statue or usurp a painted tomb and make it his own, and it is no coincidence that many of the statues inscribed with the name of the Nineteenth Dynasty king Ramesses II bear an uncanny resemblance to the statues of Amenhotep III. In all cases, by adding the new name the image became that new person. The original owner, who may have been relying on the image to serve as a link between the living and the dead, was left bereft.

Egypt's artists had list of long-established conventions to follow. Human figures had to be created according to a 'canon of proportions', and for most of the Eighteenth Dynasty a real or theoretical grid was used to ensure that, in any particular scene, seated figures consistently measured fourteen squares from the bottom of the foot to the brow while standing figures measured eighteen squares. During the Amarna Period, when the presence of the Aten shining high in the sky drew the eye upwards, these proportions were adjusted, with the body above the navel being lengthened so that the legs appeared short in comparison to the torso. The emphasised head and the hips initially appeared out of proportion but were quickly readjusted to give a more natural effect. At the same time the fingers were lengthened, and the artists started to differentiate between left and right hands.[16]

Artists were tasked with representing the three-dimensional

world on a flat surface, and at a reduced scale. They did not use perspective, shadowing or foreshortening; instead, their conceptual art was designed to represent the exact nature of a thing or person in the simplest way possible, in the same way that young children's art sets out to show the essential features of its subject.[17] To achieve this, the subject was shown diagrammatically, with the head in profile, the shoulders and torso facing forward and the legs and feet again in profile. This uncomfortable pose ensured that the essential characteristics of the subject were obvious, so that if the reanimated image ever needed to serve as a home for the soul, both limbs and body parts could be utilised to maximum effect. However, it did cause some problems. Many ancient Egyptians faced the afterlife with two left feet, or two right hands, and everyone had just one eye and one nipple.

The rigid application of these rules caused the distinctive dynastic style which allows the non-expert to identify a carved or painted figure as an Egyptian king and which, perhaps, distracts that same non-expert from noticing subtle differences in presentation when they do creep in. At first glance, an image of a Ptolemaic king does not look too dissimilar to an image of an Old Kingdom king, even though the two may be separated by twenty-five centuries. So, writing in 1764 at a time when few of his readers would have had the opportunity to view any Egyptian image or artefact, the influential Prussian art historian Johann Joachim Winckelmann felt comfortable in explaining to his readers that Egyptian art, although technically accomplished, was effectively stagnant:

> *The art of drawing amongst the Egyptians is to be compared to a tree which, though well cultivated, has been checked and arrested in its growth by a worm, or other casualties; for it remained unchanged, precisely the same, yet without attaining its perfection, until the period when Greek kings held sway over them.*[18]

Winckelmann's harsh analysis was completely in line with contemporary thinking. Dynastic Egypt has always fascinated Western observers, and its influence can be seen in art, architecture and design stretching from the days of ancient Rome to the present day. But in the eighteenth century, the origins of Western civilisation were believed to be firmly rooted in the classical world, while the sculptures of the classical world were regarded as perfection in stone. The more static Egyptian statues fell well short of this ideal. Winckelmann was writing in the hope that contemporary baroque artists might be persuaded to reach back to the excellence of ancient Greece, and develop a neo-classicism for his own age.[19] For him, and for many others, Egypt was a cultural dead end, its quaint hieroglyphic texts unreadable and its art beautifully decorative but essentially meaningless. Museums reflected this view, displaying their sparse Egyptology collections as curiosities to entertain rather than educate.[20]

This attitude gradually started to change as, following Napoleon's 1798 Egyptian campaign, illustrated books and expanding museum collections brought ancient Egypt to a wider Western audience. In 1822 the decoding of the hieroglyphic script made Egypt's long history obvious, and kick-started Egyptology as the academic discipline that we know today. As the ancient Egyptians shed their undeserved reputation as an animal worshipping, incestuous and essentially primitive people, it became clear that their 'expressionless' sculpture incorporated a multitude of subtle messages, and that their 'failure' to employ perspective in two-dimensional art was an entirely valid choice. Occasional finds of non-royal sculptures executed in a lively manner showed that Egypt's sculptors could compete with the best of the classical sculptors when they wanted to. Egyptian portraiture, far from suffering from Winckelmann's 'arrested growth', is now accepted as exhibiting a surprising modernity. Egyptologist Jan Assmann sums up this new appreciation:

Egyptian portraiture ranks among the most enigmatic and amazing challenges which history has in store for us. The enigma does not lie in the fact of its remoteness and strangeness, but quite to the contrary in its very closeness, its seeming familiarity and modernity ... The bust of queen Nefertiti from the Amarna Period ... was, after its discovery, immediately welcomed into the world of Helena Rubenstein and Elizabeth Arden, where it decorates the windows of innumerable beauty salons.[21]

But the old attitudes lingered. When, in 1823 the British Museum acquired a colossal head believed to be of 'Orus', but later revealed to be Amenhotep III, Peter Patmore's *Guide to the Beauties of the British Museum* classified it as beautiful, and undeniably well made, yet somehow lacking in true artistic merit:

It also [he has just described the Younger Memnon head of Ramesses II as lacking in life, character and expression 'like a beautiful mask'] possesses the same characteristic want of character. It is, in fact, a block of granite cut into the representation of a human face, but without any individual expression whatever; and even without any sexual expression. It has a national character, but nothing more.[22]

This approach was to affect the development of the museum's Egyptology collection, which in turn affected the public perception of Egyptian art. When, during his 1893/4 season of excavation at the site of Koptos (modern Quft), Flinders Petrie discovered three colossal limestone sculptures in the ancient temple of the fertility god Min, he recognised them as an important stage in the evolution of Egyptian cult statues.[23] With an estimated date of 3300 BCE, the three Mins stood amongst the world's earliest sculptures, but the British Museum was unimpressed and rejected his offer of two of the statues on the grounds that they were 'unhistoric rather than prehistoric'. The Ashmolean Museum, in contrast, was very impressed, and gladly accepted them.[24] They remain on display in Oxford today.

An Evolving Image

If we take a closer look at our stone pharaohs we see that, of course, in spite of the acceptance of an ideal royal form, Egypt's kings were not identical. Over 3,000 years of images reveal subtle and cumulative variations on the basic theme caused by different workshop styles, different raw materials, different tools, different fashions and, most importantly, different expectations and beliefs. Broadly speaking, the pyramid-building monarchs of the Old Kingdom (c.2686–2160 BCE) were carved to resemble remote, god-like creatures while the Middle Kingdom pharaohs (c.2055–1650 BCE) retained the athletic bodies of their predecessors but were given careworn, almost gaunt faces, and were often equipped with large ears, which may have been a family trait but which are more likely to represent their willingness to listen to both their subjects and their gods. The kings of the earlier Eighteenth Dynasty, the first dynasty of the New Kingdom, display modest ears and the confident demeanour of successful warriors and builders. This is reflected in their broad shoulders, low waists and muscular yet elegant bodies, and in their calm, almost smiling faces. None of these kings is identical and, although we may be tempted to think that this is merely a reflection of different workshop styles, is interesting to note that Hatshepsut and Tuthmosis III, who reigned alongside each other for twenty-two years when they presumably employed the same workshops, have similarly youthful faces but subtly different bodies, with Hatshepsut appearing more slender and having longer legs.

Returning to the 'characterless' British Museum head of Amen-hotep so quickly dismissed by Patmore, our knowledge of ancient Egypt in general, and Egyptian art in particular, allows us to see a proud and successful king whose very ability to create such an impressive hard stone image reinforces the fact that he is ruling with the blessing of the gods. Beneath his blue crown, Amenhotep's rounded face displays a wealth of personal features: almond-shaped eyes set at a slightly oblique angle, a broad-based snubbed nose and well-defined almost pursed full lips, the upper thicker than the lower, possibly concealing an overbite. Two-dimensional scenes in the Luxor Temple allow us to observe Amenhotep's body as he grows from youth to maturity and old age.[25] Initially his figure differs little from that of his father Tuthmosis IV, but gradually, differences start to creep in. His legs lengthen, his torso becomes shorter and thicker, and his ears are more detailed, allowing us to see that his heavy lobes have been pierced. After the celebration of his *heb-sed* jubilee, in his regnal year 30, his face develops a more youthful quality, with larger eyes. On the walls of his tomb, he appears surprisingly plump, with a thickened waist and youthful face. The *heb-sed* was an ancient ceremony designed to renew the powers of ageing kings. By the Eighteenth Dynasty it was officially celebrated after thirty years on the throne, and then every three or four years thereafter. This made it a rare celebration; few kings could hope to reign for thirty years, so surely those who did must be especially favoured by the gods? From this time onwards, we find Amenhotep increasingly drawn to the solar cults, and increasingly interested in exploring his own divinity. He now identifies himself with the sun god Re-Horakhty and, having adopted the title 'the Dazzling Aten', rules as a living manifestation of all the traditional gods.

Our final view of Amenhotep III is found on a carved stela, recovered from the Amarna house of a courtier named Panehsy.[26] Panehsy had served the royal family for a long time, and it is not unreasonable that his devotions would be performed before the old king and queen rather than the new. His stela is not particularly well executed and it has suffered considerable damage, which makes the scene far from clear. It seems to show a listless Amenhotep slumped on his throne, with Queen Tiy seated, alert and entirely conventional, beside him. Those who have chosen to read the scene literally have insisted that it depicts a shift of power:

> [T]here is every reason to suppose that queen Tiy possessed the ability to impress the claims of new thought upon her husband's mind, and gradually to turn his eyes, and those of the court, away from the sombre worship of Amon [sic] into the direction of the brilliant cult of the sun ... By the time that Amenophis III had reigned for thirty years or so, he had ceased to give much attention to state affairs, and the power had almost entirely passed into the capable hands of Tiy.[27]

It is, however, highly unlikely that any king would ever be depicted suffering or in pain; there was too great a danger that this might become an unpleasant and permanent reality in the afterlife. It is far more likely that this stela was carved at Amarna after Amenhotep's death, and that the 'ill' king is simply a king being depicted, rather clumsily, by a mason struggling with a new art style.

3

TAUGHT BY THE KING

When we consider the stupendous monuments of their labours, we can scarcely doubt, that they felt and aspired to the Sublime; but of the Beautiful, they seem to have had scarcely an idea. In Painting and in Sculpture, their taste seems at all times to have been very low and imperfect. The forms which they represented are often deficient, rude and unfinished. There is, indeed, almost universally, a kind of stiffness by which we recognise the productions of the Egyptian artists, who appear never to have remarked the beauty of the waving outline, nor the graces of its elegant and endless varieties.[1]

Edinburgh Review (1811)

As Amenhotep III fades away – his death, like almost all royal deaths, unrecorded – we start to look for signs of his successor. Just one small, seated statue seems to offer a glimpse of Akhenaten immediately after his coronation.[2] This statue was once part of a pair, but the queen who sat to the left of her husband is today represented only by a supportive arm around his back, and elements of the statue have been restored. The surviving king is perhaps plumper than we might expect, his stomach a little more prominent and his breasts a little more obvious, but he remains instantly recognisable as a later Eighteenth Dynasty Egyptian pharaoh. Unfortunately, there is nothing to confirm who he is, and although it is often assumed that he is Akhenaten he could equally well be Amenhotep III, Smenkhkare or even Tutankhamen. This piece therefore cannot be cited as evidence of Akhenaten's appearance at the start of his reign. Putting this statue to one side, some of Akhenaten's earliest images, displayed on walls in the Karnak Temple complex, resemble those of Amenhotep III. Here Akhenaten has almond-shaped eyes, a thick neck, double chin and upturned nose, and he wears the blue crown favoured by his father.[3] Before we use these images as evidence that Akhenaten started his reign with an entirely conventional appearance, however, we have to consider that these may be repurposed images of Amenhotep III.

However he may have appeared at the start of his reign, we can see that by the end of regnal year 5, immediately before the move to Amarna, Akhenaten had developed a unique style which, although he retained the regalia (crown and/or headdress, ceremonial beard, crook and flail) and clothing (kilt) which identified him as an Egyptian king, caused him to look very different from all the kings who had gone before. The colossal freestanding sandstone statues created for the Theban Gempaaten temple – created by Bak's workshop, perhaps – show Akhenaten standing straight with legs close together and arms crossing the chest to hold the crook and flail. This is a pose that should remind us of the mummified king of the dead, Osiris. But Akhenaten's features leave us with no confusion over who is being represented. He has a long, narrow head balanced on a long, thin neck, the length of his face being emphasised by his tall headdresses, his long nose, ears and chin, and his false beard. Like his father he has angled, almond-shaped eyes, but while Amenhotep's eyelids are convex, Akhenaten has sunken lids, so that he seems to peer downwards at those looking up at his face. Akhenaten also has hollow cheeks, sharp cheekbones and sensuous, plump lips with the lower lip thicker than the upper. His chin is prominent, and has variously been described as 'determined' or even 'aristocratic'. Often, two smile lines run down from the corners of his nose to his lips, and there may be wrinkles on his neck. Akhenaten's body shape is emphasised by the tight, knee-length pleated kilt that runs underneath his sagging stomach, exposing his navel. He has under-developed lower legs, strong thighs, wide hips, a well-defined waist and narrow shoulders and arms that end in long, bony fingers. His breasts, partially hidden by his crossed arms, are prominent and placed high on his chest. This same change is observable in his two-dimensional art, where it can appear even more extreme.

One Gempaaten sculpture has generated a huge amount of speculation.[4] At first glance the figure resembles the other colossal statues; it stands, lower legs and crown missing, holding the crook and flail in crossed arms. The remains of a false beard are obvious on the neck and chin. However, the statue is naked and without any obvious genitalia. Are we looking at a form of Akhenaten, who is making a bizarre attempt to combine male and female attributes in imitation of his male/female god? Or are we looking at Nefertiti, who is being allowed to assume the pose and regalia of a king?

At Thebes, the colossal Akhenatens wore a range of crowns and headdresses, including the four-feathered crown identified with the god of air, Shu. The divine triad of Shu, his sister-wife Tefnut and their father, the sun god Atum, were Egypt's first living beings. Their story is an instructive one for anyone interested in Akhenaten's beliefs.[5] It tells how, at the beginning of time, nothing existed but the waters of Nun. Deep within the waters of Nun there was an egg, which suddenly cracked open, releasing life. With a surge of energy, a mound rose out of the waters. Seated on that mound was the sun god, Atum. Atum had created himself; he now set about creating others. He grasped his penis, sneezed and spat and generated two children; Shu the god of the dry air and Tefnut the goddess of moisture. Their asexual birth is reflected the twins' names. 'Shu', derived from the Egyptian word meaning 'emptiness', sounds like the word for sneeze while the 'Tef' in Tefnut's obscure name means 'spit'. Tefnut was to give birth to two children: Geb the god of the earth and Nut the goddess of the sky, who would become the father and mother of Egypt's other deities.

Atum, the 'lord of totality', was an ancient and immensely powerful being with the ability to create and simultaneously end everything. Although his cult and mythology were to be absorbed by the cult and mythology of Re, Atum remained a potent being until the end of the dynastic age, becoming associated with the old and dying evening sun and, through this, with the dead and the afterlife. Shu and Tefnut are Egypt's first sexually differentiated beings. Shu is a life force associated with dry air, mist and sunlight who is present at all births, and he has a great capacity to heal. As the son of Atum, Egypt's first king, he is also heir to the throne. Tefnut is his queen and complement: a shadowy life force associated with moisture who might appear as a woman, a lioness or a lion-headed woman. As the daughter of the sun god she could be equated with the goddess Maat; like all solar goddesses she was fiercely loyal to her king. As Akhenaten directly equated himself with Shu, we may speculate that he also equated Nefertiti with Tefnut and his father with Atum. This means that when we see, as we often do at Amarna, a scene of Akhenaten and Nefertiti beneath the rays of the Aten, we can interpret it three ways: the royal couple worshipping their god; Shu and Tefnut standing beneath the rays of their father Atum; or maybe Akhenaten and Nefertiti worshipping Amenhotep III.

In 1858 Karl Richard Lepsius published a folio of images copied from the Amarna elite tombs and boundary stelae, and the two-dimensional version of Akhenaten's world was exposed to Western eyes.[6] Baffled by the blatant rule breaking, scholars sought practical but far-fetched explanations for what they saw. While Auguste Mariette suggested that Akhenaten (whom he knew as Khuenaten) may have been captured and castrated while leading a military campaign in Nubia, Eugène Lefèbvre favoured the theory that Akhenaten had been a 'disguised' female king, as Hatshepsut had been before him.[7] Observing the prominent and active nature of the queen and the royal daughters in the tomb scenes, many believed that Akhenaten's reign was subjected to an abnormal and unhealthy female influence. Akhenaten was a doubly unfortunate man: effeminate and under his wife's thumb. John Gardner Wilkinson, who had inspected the elite tombs first hand, suggested that the royal family must have been foreigners:

> From their features it is evident that they were not Egyptians; their omission in the list of kings, the erasure of their names, the destruction of their monuments, and the abject submission they required, prove them to have been looked on with hatred in the country; and the peculiar mode of worshipping and representing the Sun argues that their religion differed from the Egyptian.[8]

Flinders Petrie, who had gazed into the eyes of Akhenaten's 'death mask', believed that Akhenaten took after his father:

> Children are often observed to resemble one parent, and yet to grow up more like the other. To suppose that Akhenaten was like his father when a boy, and that the likeness was exaggerated as being the fashionable face – yet that as his mind and body took shape between twelve and sixteen, under the vigorous and determined

*tutelage of his imperious mother, Thyi, he should have grown into
a nearer resemblance of her ... seems not at all an unlikely state of
the case. Moreover, the cast of his head is of an expression betwixt
that of two portraits ... and links them together.*[9]

Petrie was a believer in physiognomy: the 'science' of assessing
personality and character from the face, which was popular with
many of his contemporaries. That Akhenaten's character had been
inherited from his mother was therefore confirmed for him by finds
from a sculptor's workshop 'near the south end of town':

*Two heads of an aged queen were found ... These must evidently
be of Thyi, as the face is too old and too dissimilar to be that of
Nefertiti. Here the resemblance with Akhenaten is obvious ... the
same forehead almost in line with the nose, the same dreamy eye,
the same delicate nose, the same expression of lips, the same long
chin, the same slanting neck. That the boy inherited his face from
his father ... cannot be doubted; and that he grew up like his
mother seems equally clear.*[10]

Increasing exploration at Amarna, including Davies's painstak-
ing recording and subsequent publication of the scenes decorating
the elite tombs (1903–8), made the perplexities of Akhenaten's art
more obvious and confirmed the view that this was a new realism, a
reflection of Akhenaten's devotion to *maat* which was unfortunately
interpreted as a 'desire for truth at any price'.[11] Akhenaten had
perhaps suffered from a feminising disease that affected his appearance. So, to take just one example, in 1922 we find Arthur Weigall,
a great admirer of Akhenaten, interpreting the king as

*a pale sickly youth. His head seemed too large for his body; his
eyelids were heavy; his eyes were eloquent of dreams. His features*

were delicately moulded, and his mouth, in spite of a somewhat protruding lower jaw, is reminiscent of the best of the art of Rossetti.[12]

The satirical magazine *Punch* begged to differ: 'One knows what modern artists can do in the way of distending and emaciating the figure, and early Egypt may have suffered under similar sorrows.'[13]

The vision of the sick king certainly matched the prevalent view that Akhenaten was a gentle theologian; a man more interested in religion than war, who decorated his palaces with beautiful, peaceful scenes of nature. But it did not quite fit the facts. Could such a sick man really have challenged royal tradition with such determination and vigour? Could he have fathered numerous children? As more sculptures were uncovered from both Amarna and Thebes, opinion shifted again as Egyptologists decided that the art could not be read literally. This was surely a state-sanctioned attempt to express Akhenaten's personal religious beliefs stimulated, perhaps, by the fact that the Aten, unlike Egypt's other gods, could not be depicted adequately in three-dimensional stone. With the traditional images of the king standing or sitting beside his god now an impossibility, a new form of representation was necessary. Dorothea Arnold, for example, has described how:

The somewhat aloof smile gives human expression to the Karnak statue's surprising head, but the size and shape of the head and face clearly exceed natural dimensions. We are confronted less with a representation of a human face than with artistic variations of human features. The effect is awesome: pharaoh's divinity expressed through a transfiguration of the human form.[14]

Dominic Monserrat ties the king's appearance even more firmly into his religious beliefs:

The Aten subsumes into itself all the different gods who create and maintain the universe and the king is the living image of the Aten on earth. He can therefore display on earth the Aten's multiple life-giving functions. These are represented through a set of signifiers that seem mutually contradictory to modern viewers, such as the appearance of male and female physical characteristics on the same statue, but made sense to the intended Egyptian audience. These attributes render the king literally superhuman, a divine body which goes beyond human experience.[15]

The Aten, although conventionally described as 'he', was actually a combination of male and female elements which allowed him to be the father and mother of all things. He was both asexual and androgynous, as, to a certain extent, are all of Akhenaten's statues, which combine masculine elements with the body of a woman whose soft stomach suggests that she has given birth. That the new royal image was revealed to the world as Akhenaten prepared to celebrate an unexpected *heb-sed* after a mere three years on the throne is no coincidence. The *heb-sed* allowed kings to reflect on their own relationship with their gods, and it had heralded an increase in royal divinity during the reign of Amenhotep III. This may be the point where the Aten/Atum merged with Akhenaten's father, while Akhenaten and Nefertiti became Shu and Tefnut.

Reality or symbolism? The truth probably lies somewhere between the two, with the artists exploiting and exaggerating Akhenaten's natural body shape to create an image which linked him firmly with his god. We can gain support for this idea by revisiting Tutankhamen's tomb. The garments buried with the young king were in various sizes ranging from child to adult; these were not clothes specifically made for the tomb, that the king might enjoy wearing in his afterlife, but the clothes that Tutankhamen actually wore during his ten-year reign. They allow us to calculate his vital statistics with a fair degree of accuracy. Tutankhamen's mummy confirms that he stood approximately 167.5cm tall (5ft 6in); his chest, measured from his 'mannequin', was 80cm (31in); his waist, estimated by measuring his belts, sashes and the mannequin, which we have to assume was accurate, 75cm (29in); his hips, estimated from his loincloths, 110cm (43in).[16] This is the same pear shape, with a narrow waist but heavy lower body and wide hips, which we see exaggerated in the Gempaaten colossi. As Tutankhamen became king while still a child he must have inherited his throne, rather than claimed it through marriage or conquest; this indicates that he was closely related to Akhenaten. It therefore seems that wide hips and strong thighs were a family trait.

For some this new image is ugly; even grotesque. Arnold has described the Theban colossi as 'pole-like, elongated images of an extraterrestrial being'.[17] Alan Gardiner, unable to disconnect the young king's appearance from what he knew of his subsequent behaviour, saw 'frankly hideous portraits the general fidelity of which cannot be doubted … the standing colossi from the peristyle court at Karnak have a look of fanatical determination such as his subsequent history confirmed all too fatally'.[18]

Others have found Akhenaten's face sensual, or hauntingly beautiful, particularly when, as originally intended, seen from below and lit from above. However we view it, it is very different from all royal images that have gone before, yet still instantly recognisable as an Egyptian king. Akhenaten has not abandoned the conventions, he has merely exaggerated them. This was the start of a lifelong artistic experiment. As his reign progressed, as his ideas matured and, perhaps, as Bak retired at Thebes and the Thutmose workshop came to prominence at Amarna, the official style became less extreme and more realistic. Art historian Cyril Aldred identified three distinct phases; the early style which started in Thebes and lasted until approximately regnal year 8, a transitional phase that lasted until approximately regnal year 12, and a late or final phase which includes nearly all the work recovered from Thutmose's workshop.[19] This is probably an over-rigid analysis, suggesting too much conscious planning, but essentially it is correct. Certainly, the images recovered from Thutmose's workshop demonstrate a softer and more confident realism than the images seen at Thebes. Akhenaten's face now is less haggard and his body less feminine although still, in comparison to conventional royal images, flabby and out of condition.

Introducing Nefertiti

As we suspected when we looked at Bak's naos, the new artistic style was quickly extended to Akhenaten's family and his court, who now reflected their king's altered appearance. Egyptologists initially interpreted this as a great artistic freedom:

> *For the first and last time in the history of the nation, her artists were apparently left free to depict things as they saw them, instead of being obliged to force their subjects into a conventional mould. The results of this casting-off of swaddling-bands are, as was to be expected, of very unequal merit in different hands.*[20]

This interpretation fitted well with the twentieth-century acceptance of Akhenaten as a promoter of freedom and tolerance. It is, however, entirely incorrect. We have no reason to believe that Akhenaten was a tolerant individual, and mirroring was already a common artistic conceit whereby the lesser subject flattered the more important subject by replicating his or her posture and appearance, bringing a pleasing coherence and symmetry to any scene. We should no more imagine that Akhenaten's court suddenly developed elongated faces and prominent stomachs than we would expect the elite of early twentieth-century Paris to have displayed the oval faces depicted by Modigliani, or the cube bodies painted by Picasso. Nor should we assume, as James Baikie did, that the Amarna court were all closely related:

> *Feature by feature the two sets of portraits [Akhenaten and Nefertiti] not only resemble each other, but speak beyond question of the very closest blood-relationship between their originals ... we must conclude that Nefertiti was full sister to her husband – a relationship which, however shocking it may seem to us, was regarded as a perfectly normal one by the Egyptians.*[21]

To prove that we are seeing style rather than realism, we simply need to look at individuals who were depicted before or after, as well as during, the Amarna Period. Akhenaten's mother, Tiy, is a good example. She appeared many times during her husband's reign, displaying the face and figure appropriate to an Egyptian consort. In the Amarna tomb of her steward Huya, however, she has the same angular body and relaxed posture as her son. Tiy's young granddaughter, Ankhesenpaaten, shares this body shape at Amarna, where she has an exaggeratedly elongated, egg-shaped head, yet when she becomes Ankhesenamen, consort of Tutankhamen, her head has a more natural shape.

To disprove the suggestion that Akhenaten and Nefertiti were brother and sister, we need to consider Nefertiti's titles. Nefertiti never names her parents but we would not expect her to. Her status at court was entirely dependent on her union with the king, and in this respect her parents were irrelevant. However, the fact that she never calls herself 'King's Daughter' (the equivalent of our 'princess') confirms that she was commoner-born. Royal titles were cumulative, and rather than drop an earlier title on her marriage, she would have progressed to become a 'King's Daughter, King's Great Wife'.

Similarly her sister Mutnodjmet, who appears as a companion to the young princesses in several elite tomb scenes, fails to use any royal title.

In picking a non-royal consort, Akhenaten had followed the very successful precedent set by his father, who made no secret of the fact that he had chosen a non-royal consort: 'Amenhotep ruler of Thebes, given life, and the king's principal wife Tiy, may she live. The name of her father is Yuya and the name of her mother is Thuyu; she is the wife of a mighty king.'[22]

Circumstantial evidence would suggest that Nefertiti was born into Tiy's birth family. In the Amarna tomb of Ay and his wife Tey, Tey is identified as the 'favourite of the Good God, nurse of the King's Great Wife Nefertiti, nurse of the goddess, ornament of the king': it seems that she raised the infant Nefertiti, maybe as her foster-mother or stepmother.[23] Meanwhile Ay's many titles include the positions of 'overseer of the king's horses' and 'God's Father'. Yuya, father of Tiy, bore the same titles. Could Ay have inherited his titles from his father, Yuya? This would mean that he was Akhenaten's maternal uncle. Did, as Borchardt suggested, 'God's Father' mean 'king's father-in-law'?[24] Ay himself makes no mention of any connection to Nefertiti but that is not unexpected; Yuya makes no reference to his daughter Queen Tiy and, if we did not have the 'marriage scarab' issued by Amenhotep III, we would not properly understand their relationship.

Our first sighting of the new queen comes from the elite cemeteries on the west bank of the Nile, at Thebes. As Akhenaten came to the throne, the court official Parennefer was engaged in decorating his rock-cut tomb.[25] Today his tomb is in a bad state of repair and it is very difficult to make sense of the surviving artwork. But when Norman de Garis Davis visited in 1923, he was able to identify a scene on the facade which included the image of an unnamed lady, almost certainly Nefertiti, who accompanied the king (identified as

Amenhotep IV) as he worshipped the Aten. Davies describes the queen as (probably) wearing a modius or platform crown topped by two tall feathers, and carrying two sistra. An interior scene, now completely destroyed, showed the same lady sitting on a chair beside the enthroned king as he received Parennefer and rewarded him for his loyalty. This tomb, it seems, made reference to the new king and queen yet was decorated using the traditional art style.

The unfinished Theban tomb of the vizier Ramose is partially decorated in the old art style and partially in the new. It offers a much clearer view of the lady whom we can now with confidence identify as Nefertiti.[26] Once again a loyal tomb owner is being recognised by his king. This time Akhenaten stands at the palace balcony known as the 'Window of Appearances'. As he leans forward to reward the faithful Ramose with gold, Nefertiti stands passively behind him, holding a fly-whisk in her left hand. The scene is only partially carved, and both king and queen are hidden from the waist downwards by the palace wall. However, we can see that while Nefertiti has a conventionally slender upper body, she has a prominent jaw which mirrors Akhenaten's own. She is dressed in a pleated linen robe with sleeves, and her head is covered by a short bobbed wig and the uraeus or rearing snake headdress which signifies royalty.

Our clearest view of the Theban Nefertiti comes from the walls of the Benben Temple (*Hwt bnbn*); a companion temple to Akhenaten's Gempaaten. Here, reconstructed scenes show Nefertiti offering to the Aten, assisted by her eldest daughter Meritaten. Nefertiti appears as a thin and angular woman wearing an elaborate pleated gown and a Hathor-style crown perched on top of a long wig. Meritaten, depicted as a miniature Nefertiti rather than a child, carries a sistrum, the religious rattle often associated with the cult of Hathor. The Aten, as always, shines high in the sky, his rays extending their blessing over the queen and her daughter. These images are often cited as proof that Nefertiti was, even at the start of her husband's reign, allowed to usurp the king's priestly role. The situation is, however, less clear cut than has been supposed.

It is true that in normal circumstances we would expect to see the king making all the offerings in any state temple. In non-royal contexts too, it is rare to see a woman acting as the primary contact with a deity, because this role was traditionally reserved for a man. Only when her husband was absent, was a woman allowed to perform this function. However, if the Benben Temple was dedicated to purely female rites, it would not be a normal state temple, and the normal rules would not apply. It may well be that Akhenaten is absent because, if he were present, he would block Nefertiti's access to the god.[27] We could usefully compare Nefertiti's work in the Benben Temple to the rituals traditionally performed by the earlier Eighteenth Dynasty God's Wives of Amen. The role of 'God's Wife' was traditionally reserved for the principal queen or queen mother. On the walls of Hatshepsut's Red Chapel at Karnak we can see a God's Wife, in this case Hatshepsut's daughter, Neferure, in action.[28] In one scene she is shown performing a ritual to burn and destroy the name of Egypt's enemies, while in another she stands, arms raised, to watch Hatshepsut present the seventeen gods of Karnak with their dinner. A third scene shows the God's Wife leading a group of priests to the temple pool to be purified, and then following Hatshepsut into the sanctuary, where the king performs rites before the statue of Amen.

Nefertiti's face continues to evolve throughout her husband's reign until, before his regnal year 12, she loses her drooping jaw and chin and acquires a square jaw, prominent cheekbones, rounded cheeks and straighter lips.[29] At the same time the proportions of her head and neck are adjusted to give a more natural appearance. Her body changes too, so that while she maintains her well-defined waist and unremarkable breasts (obvious breasts not being an exclusively female trait at Amarna), she develops a rounded abdomen, wide hips and thighs and pronounced buttocks. Her stomach is often highlighted by a single curved line just above the pubic mound while her mother-in-law has two such lines plus a double line under each breast. Nefertiti's dresses, either a delicate, pleated robe which is often left completely open (perhaps we are missing the painted undergarment?) or a close-fitting linen dress, make her body shape very obvious.

When Jan Assmann writes 'The statues of Nefertiti may be regarded as love-poems in stone ... there is a very refined sensuousness and an almost erotic grace and radiance in the art of this period,' he is writing quite literally.[30] The handful of surviving New Kingdom love poems betray an admiration for the same long neck, slim waist, wide hips and heavy thighs that we see in Nefertiti's images. The queen has been given, in somewhat exaggerated form, the body of an alluring woman. This will have been important to Akhenaten. As the self-proclaimed son of the sun god he needed a mate who would stimulate his own sexual prowess just as Tefnut had stimulated Shu. It can be difficult for us to determine the extent to which the Egyptian artists used a visual code to convey this sexual message.[31] We understand that the wives depicted in private male tombs always appear healthy, young and fertile because a sexually active wife will assist her husband's own rebirth. But does every scene showing Nefertiti with her husband carry a similar hidden meaning? Is every scene of Akhenaten, Nefertiti and their daughters intended to remind us of the king's fertility?

We have more images of Nefertiti than of any other queen consort. This prominence goes unexplained in the written texts, leaving us to guess the extent to which this is the result of more of Akhenaten's art being preserved (albeit in pieces); a reflection of Akhenaten's need to have his consort and daughters take the place of the discredited traditional gods; an indication of Nefertiti's atypically high personal status; or a combination of all these and more.

Because we have more images, we see more of Nefertiti in action; this gives the impression that she does more than any previous consort, and this in turn suggests that she is more important. Claims that Nefertiti 'was accorded an exalted status unparalleled for a King's Great Wife during the history of dynastic Egypt' are commonly made, but very difficult to confirm.[32] Before we can decide that Nefertiti is indeed uniquely prominent amongst all of Egypt's consorts, we need to give some consideration to the role played by her mother-in-law and predecessor, Tiy.

The queen consorts of the late Seventeenth and earlier Eighteenth Dynasties had been accomplished women with a strong religious and political presence. Ahhotep, the widowed mother of Ahmose I, for example, had served as regent for her young son and was subsequently celebrated as one who 'pacified Upper Egypt and expelled her rebels'. Her daughter Ahmose-Nefertari bore a string of religious titles, helped her son Amenhotep I with his rule and was eventually deified at Deir el-Medina, where her cult flourished until the end of the New Kingdom.[33] All this was entirely in line with the accepted duties of the consort, who was expected to support her husband, protect his children, perform specific female-based religious rites and, if necessary, deputise for the absent or dead king. However, following the reign of the female pharaoh Hatshepsut, and perhaps as a backlash against it, subsequent consorts had semi-retired from public gaze. We know their names, but can say little about them.

Tiy reversed this trend, maintaining a high public profile throughout her marriage. She was depicted alongside Amenhotep on public monuments and in private tombs, and her name was linked with his on official inscriptions and in diplomatic correspondence, so that her reputation spread throughout the empire. A letter of condolence written by Tushratta of Mitanni following Amenhotep's death, confirms that Tiy's influence continued into her son's reign:

You know that I always showed love to Nimmuaria [Amenhotep III], your husband, and that Nimmuaria your husband always showed love to me ... I had asked your husband for statues of solid gold ... But now Napkhururiya, your son, has sent plated statues of wood. With gold being as dirt in your son's land, why has your son not given what I asked for?[34]

Tiy was closely identified with the solar deities Maat and Hathor, and she became the first queen to add Hathor's cow horns and sun disc to her tall, feathered crown. The only prominent religious role that she did not play was that of God's Wife of Amen, an omission that may suggest that Amen of Thebes was already out of favour with the royal family.

Mortal women who married divine kings acquired their own patina of divinity. In the Theban tomb built for Kheruef, courtier to Amenhotep III, we can see the living Queen Tiy sailing, godlike, behind her husband in the night boat of Re.[35] Outside Egypt, this living divinity was made more obvious, and Tiy was worshipped as a form of Hathor-Tefnut at the Nubian temple of Sedeinga. Here we can see Tiy assuming the form of a sphinx to prowl across the temple pillars. If we return to Kheruef's tomb, we see Tiy sitting beside her husband as they celebrate his third jubilee. The side of her throne, which is smaller but more ornate than Amenhotep's plain seat, bears an image of Tiy as a human-headed sphinx, trampling two bound female prisoners.[36] A third sphinx image, believed to be Tiy, was found on a carved carnelian bracelet plaque recovered from Thebes. Here we see a crouched, human-headed, winged female sphinx wearing Tefnut's distinctive plant-topped headdress (a symbol of rejuvenation and fertility, perhaps) and holding Amenhotep's cartouche.[37]

It is undeniable that both Tiy and Nefertiti were allocated religious and political power, with Tiy (mentioned in diplomatic correspondence; Nefertiti, as far as we know, was not) perhaps winning in the political sphere and Nefertiti (offering in temples; Tiy, as far as we know, did not) the religious one. As far as we know, neither queen ever demonstrated a power that was equal to, or higher than, the power of the king. Can we state that Nefertiti was uniquely powerful? On this evidence, no. This is a contentious subject that we will be revisiting in Chapter 8.

4

THE BEAUTIFUL WOMAN

Nefertiti herself must have been an unusually beautiful and graceful woman.[1]

James Baikie (1926)

The Nefertiti bust is the only substantially complete work of art to be recovered from Thutmose's compound. Standing 48cm (19in) tall and weighing a hefty 20kg (44lb), it shows the head, neck and an area extending from the clavicle to just above the breasts of a woman whose hairless head is topped by a crown, and whose long, slender neck is encircled by a colourful floral collar incorporating petals and small fruits. The woman has a narrow face with prominent brow ridges and cheekbones, a long nose and full lips. Her eyes are almond shaped, her brows well defined and her chin firm. The bust has been created from carved limestone (calcium carbonate) – an unexceptional stone – coated with layers of gypsum plaster (calcium hydroxide) and painted, so that the core itself is invisible to the naked eye.

The bust is uninscribed, and so our identification of its subject is based purely on our recognition of its tall, flat-topped crown as a headdress that is unique to Nefertiti. We see this crown repeatedly in Amarna art and sculpture, and every time we see it we identify the wearer as Nefertiti, just as we identify any Amarna woman wearing large, round earrings as Kiya. This identification of people by their accessories is not ideal; if we were ever to discover that Nefertiti and Kiya shared their wardrobes we would seriously have to reconsider many of our interpretations of Amarna scenes. The extent to which we automatically associate this particular crown with Nefertiti was made clear to me when artist Aakheperure sent me a sketch showing me wearing the same crown, and I did not instantly recognise just who was being depicted. Even my family, who see my face far more often than I do, had a moment's hesitation before seeing me, rather than Nefertiti.[2]

The Berlin version of Nefertiti's tall crown is dark blue, with a uraeus (now missing) rearing over the forehead and a multicoloured band or ribbon circling the crown and tying at the back. Two colourful ribbons hang from the nape of the neck; these have an undulating outline that suggests they were made from a flimsy material, and this is confirmed by 2D scenes that show the loose ribbons fluttering in the breeze. The crown fits, bonnet-style, close to the head with a gold forehead band and back band, and is usually worn without a wig. Other images show the same basic crown decorated with varying arrangements of discs and ornaments. The origins of the crown are obscure, although its shape and colour suggest that it may have developed as a female version of the blue war crown worn by many of Egypt's kings.[3] Akhenaten himself favoured a rather high, narrow version of the blue crown, which he often decorated with stylised discs or multiple uraei, and this is what his own bust is wearing. In shape, Nefertiti's tall crown is reminiscent of the headdress worn by Tefnut, and by Tiy as a cartouche-bearing sphinx. After Nefertiti's death Mutnodjmet, consort to Horemheb and, perhaps, sister to Nefertiti, occasionally wears a crown with a similar silhouette.

Both Nefertiti and Akhenaten exhibit a variety of crowns, leading us to assume that while crowns in general separated the royals from their subjects, each crown was invested with its own specific symbolism and meaning. At Thebes, at the start of her husband's reign, we see Nefertiti wearing the single or double uraeus over a long, heavy wig, which was often topped by the tall feathered crown ornamented with the cow horns and disc introduced by Tiy. By the time she moves to Amarna Nefertiti is also wearing the tall blue crown, which she will wear with increasing frequency. Another innovation at this time is the 'cap crown'; a close-fitting bonnet decorated with a uraeus and a ribbon or band at the base, which is sometimes mistaken for the tall blue crown. The cap crown will also be worn by queens Meritaten and Ankhesenpaaten (as Tutankhamen's wife Ankhesenamen) and, in post-Amarna times, will be worn by Ramesside kings.[4] Nefertiti occasionally wears the *khat* headcloth, a bag-like head cover usually worn by kings but also worn by Tiy, and by the goddesses Isis and Nephthys. We never, however, see Nefertiti wearing Akhenaten's crown, and our only view of her wearing anything resembling a king's crown comes from the Amarna tomb of Panehsy.[5] Here Nefertiti wears a *khat* head-cloth topped by an ornate *atef* crown; a crown that, during the New Kingdom, incorporated ostrich feathers, ram and bull horns, a solar disc and multiple uraei. She stands behind a larger-scale Akhenaten, who wears a *nemes* head-cloth and an even more elaborate *atef* including two extra cobras and three additional falcons.[6] Akhenaten's crown is larger, has more elements, and appears far more regal than Nefertiti's; there is nothing here to suggest that the king and queen have equal status. This whole scene is, however, curious, as the *atef* was primarily associated with the cult of Osiris, a god who was not welcome at Amarna.

Important though they obviously were, not one of Egypt's crowns has survived. This could be explained by the fact that we have only one substantially intact royal burial representing the entire 3,000 years of the dynastic age. It could be that Tutankhamen's tomb is unrepresentative, and that other royal burials were packed floor to ceiling with different types of royal crowns. Even so, it is curious that all the crowns, along with all trace of their manufacture, should entirely vanish. It may be that we are overestimating the numbers. That there was just one set of crowns, passed from king to king and consort to consort as the dynastic age progressed, or that each king and queen had a personal set of crowns which was destroyed at their death. However, rather than attempt to track the missing crowns, we should perhaps be asking whether these crowns ever existed in the first place. Egypt is, after all, a land where art is writing and writing is art. Could the crowns simply be symbols of authority and religious power? The equivalent, perhaps, of the nimbus or circle of light and flame which artists from various cultures have traditionally used to distinguish holy and sacred people, rulers and heroes. This would certainly explain the elaborate structure of a crown such as the *atef*, which, were it made of metal or leather, would have been difficult to manufacture and heavy to wear. A parallel can be drawn here with the 'perfume cones' which are often seen on the heads of banqueters in New Kingdom tomb scenes. Early Egyptologists identified these as party hats made of scented fat. The theory was that they would melt in the heat of the banquet, releasing a pleasant odour and a cooling trickle of grease. This, however, would have been very difficult to accomplish in a land without refrigeration, and Egyptologists today are more inclined to read the cones as symbols representing scent, or happiness, or maybe death.[7]

The Bodiless Head

Because the bust has a smooth base that allows it to stand firm, we can be confident that it is a complete artefact and not simply a head that has snapped off a larger statue. Instinctively, this seems wrong. Everything that we know about Egyptian art tells us that the sculptor would always show his subject complete. The creation of a bust – a bodiless, limbless head – would have been dangerous because it left its subject open to the possibility of an uncomfortable eternity spent as a disconnected head. Yet Thutmose's workshop yielded two completed part-royals – the Nefertiti bust and its companion Akhenaten bust – plus what appears to be the lower part of a third bust, while the Louvre houses a second Akhenaten bust.[8]

Borchardt recorded the finding of the Akhenaten bust in his official excavation diary:

> In the corner room of the house, at the NE corner ... there is a life sized coloured royal bust, broken into 5 pieces, not quite complete. Face unfortunately quite battered. The following preserved: chest, piece of arm, neck, face and wog [crown].[9]

Later that same day, when Nefertiti emerged virtually intact, he regarded the two busts as a pair.

The damage to the Akhenaten bust appears to have been deliberate rather than accidental. Although it has been suggested that the bust was smashed before it was placed in the pantry, this raises the question why anyone would have bothered to save the pieces.[10] It is possible that they were collected and stored by someone loyal to Akhenaten, or by someone with a personal devotion to this particular statue, but these seem unlikely explanations, as whoever filled the pantry was preparing to abandon Amarna at a time when Akhenaten himself no longer served as a conduit to the divine. Friederike

Seyfried, current director of the Egyptian Museum and Papyrus Collection in Berlin, has pointed out that the bust shows small, neat chisel marks; evidence, perhaps, that Thutmose's workmen systematically and carefully removed the valuable gold that had been applied as part of the finish, before placing it in the pantry. This indicates that the bust was attacked some time after Thutmose's departure, by those who scoured Amarna looking for images of the king. Nefertiti's bust, further back in the room and less obvious, simply went unnoticed.[11]

If we look outside Amarna we can see that, while the creation of a bodiless head was not without precedent, it was rare. To find Egypt's earliest examples we have to go back over 1,000 years to the Old Kingdom when, for a short period of time, the burial shafts of some elite mastaba tombs included what Egyptologists have termed 'reserve heads': unpainted and uninscribed sculpted heads and necks whose flat bases allow them to stand upright.[12] These heads, a mixture of male and female, are all bald, presumably because they have removed their wigs to reveal their shaven heads. They appear so lifelike that it has been suggested that they are individual portraits, rather than off-the-peg purchases. While most of the heads are carved from fine limestone there are also crude examples incorporating moulded plaster, and even two made from mud. Of the thirty-one known reserve heads, twenty-seven have been recovered from the Giza cemetery; they mostly date to the Fourth Dynasty reigns of the Great Pyramid builder Khufu (c.2589–2566 BCE) and his son Khaefre (c.2558–2532 BCE). Many show damaged ears and several have an unexplained cut down the back of the head.

Their provenance and restricted time-span offer a clue to their purpose. All the reserve heads were recovered from tombs that, although they had a small offering chapel attached to the solid superstructure, did not have a room large enough or secure enough to house a complete statue. As mummification was at a very early stage during the Fourth Dynasty, the survival of the corpse could never be guaranteed. Yet the survival of the corpse in a recognisable state was already regarded as essential for the continued existence of the soul after death. We can therefore speculate that the reserve heads, although not ideal, were provided to serve as an emergency home for the bodiless soul. When the mastaba tombs developed secure interior chapels the reserve heads were replaced by full statues. Although Nefertiti's bust is also hairless, and has damaged ears, it seems highly unlikely that it is the Amarna equivalent of a Fourth Dynasty reserve head. Nefertiti was well represented at Amarna, at Thebes, and presumably elsewhere in Egypt. If her soul ever needed to find a substitute body, it would be spoiled for choice. More specifically, the bust is one of a pair that presumably had an identical purpose. We cannot be certain that Nefertiti died before Amarna was abandoned but we can be certain that Akhenaten did; we know that he was buried in the royal tomb. We would have expected his reserve head – if that is what his bust was – to have been included in his tomb.

The reserve heads were not the only limbless, bodiless sculptures to be buried with the dead. Tutankhamen's tomb has provided two examples. From the debris blocking the passageway leading to the anteroom came a near life-sized wooden, plastered and painted head representing Tutankhamen as the sun god Re emerging from a lotus blossom at the beginning of the world.[13] This piece tells a well-known story and, although it bears Tutankhamen's features, it is not technically a representation of the king but of the god who bears the king's face. Of more relevance to our search for a parallel to the Nefertiti bust is a wooden, plastered and painted life-sized model of an armless upper body found in the antechamber. The model is dressed in a simple white robe and wears a flat-topped crown decorated with a single uraeus. Egyptologist turned journalist Arthur Weigall caught a glimpse of the model as it was carried from the tomb, and identified it as Tutankhamen's wife Ankhesenamen (formerly Ankhesenpaaten) wearing a crown similar to that worn by her mother Nefertiti.[14] His identification was picked up by his fellow journalists, and the model entered the public imagination as a mystery woman:

> *wreathed in a glowing Mona Lisa smile – a smile which captivated the few spectators who remained at the tomb … The lips are full, the eyes dark and large, but the whites of the eyes are very pronounced. Finally the cheeks are almost certainly those of a young girl.*[15]

Howard Carter took a more practical approach, identifying the model as a male mannequin – a replica Tutankhamen – used to display the king's clothes and jewellery:

> *The most novel, perhaps, among all the antiquities seen today was a wooden dummy upon which it is believed Tutankhamen tries his tunic and other vestments, after the fashion of a modern dressmaker. Mr Henry Burton, of the New York Metropolitan Museum of Art, who is an enthusiastic member of Mr Carter's staff, advanced the opinion that Tutankhamen was a man of fashion, scrupulously exact in the fit and hang of his garments.*[16]

While Carter's identification seems unlikely – surely it would have been more useful, for a kilt-wearing king, to create a full body mannequin with legs but without an integral crown, if this was its purpose? – no one has been able to suggest a better one. All that we can conclude is that the 'mannequin', whatever its purpose, was not considered threatening to the king's well-being after death.

Although most stone sculpture is inscribed with the name and titles of the subject, Nefertiti's bust is silent. It may simply be that

Nefertiti needed no inscription – that her unique crown made her identity obvious to all – but it could be argued that her bust was not inscribed because it was intended to be just one element in a much larger, composite sculpture. Egypt's artists did not traditionally create stone statues with multiple parts, but Thutmose's Amarna compound has yielded enough complete or near-complete stone body parts, mainly heads, but also arms, hands, feet and part of a stone wig, to show that his sculptors were experimenting with this style.[17] They were not the only ones. A neighbouring sculptor's workshop (O47,16a and 20) yielded an unfinished quartzite head of Nefertiti which would have formed part of a composite statue, while a third workshop to the south of the Thutmose workshop (P 49.6) yielded an arm and a pair of hands.[18] In a city with an insatiable demand for royal statuary, this made good commercial sense. A composite statue could be manufactured quickly by different experts using relatively small blocks of stone, then transported with relative ease and assembled in situ. As an added bonus, the sculptor would be able to match individual body part to their ideal stone. So, yellow, brown or red could be used for hands, feet and heads. Black could be used for hair, eyebrows and occasionally skin, while white could be used for bodies draped in white linen. A statue made in this fashion would retain its original colours in a way that a plastered and painted statue would not. At the same time, a limestone statue with hard stone extremities would be both easier and cheaper to make than an entirely hard stone statue. However, in spite of these obvious advantages, it seems that the experiment failed, as the manufacture of composite statues largely died out at the end of the Amarna Period.

One piece recovered from the Thutmose workshop is of particular interest here. A brown quartzite head, unfinished, unpolished and still decorated with the black ink lines that would have guided the sculptor, bears a strong facial resemblance to the Nefertiti bust.[19]

This head was clearly not created as a stand-alone piece; it would have been part of a composite statue with, perhaps, a blue faience crown attached to the peg which survives on the top of the head. Although there are signs of faience working within the Thutmose workshop, there is no sign of the crown. The bodies and legs which would have made the Thutmose limb collection whole are also missing – perhaps they were made elsewhere – and, as not one composite stone statue has survived the vandalism that occurred at the end of the Amarna Period, our understanding of this innovative technique is based on theory rather than observation. We can see that heads created as part of a composite statue usually have a rounded tenon or projection at the base of the neck; this would have slotted into a mortise or hole on the torso. The joint would then be glued firm using a mixture of resin and powdered stone coloured to disguise the seam. As the wig or crown would have been a separate piece there is often a second tenon on the head. However, the Amarna princesses, whose exaggeratedly egg-shaped heads were not hidden under wigs or crowns, lack this second tenon.

The mortise-and-tenon would not have been the strongest joint to use when creating a large, heavy, stone statue. It was, however, the joint already being used in the creation of wooden statues, suggesting that Thutmose's workforce copied their technique unvaryingly from the carpenter's workshop. We can draw a useful parallel here with one of the Amarna Period's best-recognised 'portraits': a small wooden head of Tiy recovered from Gurob, the site of an extensive Eighteenth Dynasty harem palace.[20] This head measures just 22.5cm (9in) including its tall headdress, and is carved from three different types of wood. Unusually, it allows us to see Tiy not as a stereotypical ageless queen, but as a real, elderly woman with downturned lips, heavy eyelids, almond-shaped eyes and deep lines running from her nose to her mouth. She currently wears a bobbed, round wig made of linen and covered in blue glass beads, but it is clear that her head was remodelled in antiquity, as beneath this wig we can see remains of an earlier bag-like *khat* headdress, a pair of gold earrings and four golden uraei. Confirming that the head is part of a composite statue, it has a neck tenon which would have allowed it to be inserted into a torso, while a second tenon, on the head, allowed the attachment of a modius headdress and tall double plumes which, once separated, have recently been reattached by museum conservators. The headdress links Tiy with the goddesses Hathor and Isis and suggests, perhaps, that either the statue or the queen has been deified.

The care lavished on Tiy's small head dispels any suggestion that a wooden statue was considered a cheap or inferior option. Beyond confirming the importance attached to the statue, the significance of the queen's change in regalia is hard for us to assess, but it is possible that it coincides with Tiy's developing role in Akhenaten's religion. He would not be the first king to use his mother to stress a very personal link with the gods; indeed, his own father, Amenhotep III, had used the walls of the Luxor Temple to tell the story of his divine birth as the son of Amen-Re and the secondary queen Mutemwia. If Akhenaten felt himself to be the son of a divine being his mother, as a woman who has communicated with that divine being, must surely have been allowed her own share of divinity.

Although we know that Thutmose's workers were experimenting with the composite style, it is unlikely that the Nefertiti bust was ever intended for insertion into a torso. The presence of the finished shoulders, the absence of a tenon for attachment and the fact that the crown is integral to the piece all suggest that it is a work of art in its own right. Nevertheless, a highly controversial modern art installation has shown that it would, theoretically, have been possible to unite the bust with a body. In 2002 the artists known as Little Warsaw (András Gálik and Bálint Havas) developed *The Body of Nefertiti* for display in the Hungarian Pavilion at the 50th Venice

Biennale (2003). Their inspiration was the redisplay of popular and historical symbols in contemporary contexts, establishing a connection between the present and the temporality of art and so demonstrating the continuity of culture. Nefertiti, as perhaps the best known symbol from the ancient world, was an obvious subject for their work. They did not see her primarily as a symbol of Africa, but of Europe:

> *This statue is one of the important sources of European cultural history and sculpture, even though it was created outside the continent. Its outsider position adds further meaning to the project of completing: this 3000 years old model has been contributing, ever since it was found and put on display, to the European ideal of beauty.*[21]

Their original intention was to create a metal body, unite it with the bust and display the composite statue in Venice. However, the museum authorities refused permission for the bust to travel. Undaunted, Little Warsaw created a life-sized, and rather modern looking, bronze body for Nefertiti. At first sight their body seems to be naked, though it is actually wrapped in a diaphanous linen robe. The body was taken to Berlin, where it was placed near the case displaying Nefertiti's head. Then, for a few hours on 26 May 2003, the ancient head became one with its modern body:

> *The idea was to create a headless statue that alludes to Nefertiti but is a distinct and separate work of art ... the headless sculpture in Venice holds the memory of the earlier encounter with the Egyptian head in Berlin.*[22]

This brief union was filmed, and the film subsequently displayed alongside the headless torso in the Hungarian Pavilion in Venice.

It can have come as no surprise to anyone that the decision to allow the bust to be used in this way, although fiercely defended by the museum as a legitimate artistic experiment, sparked angry demands that it be returned to Cairo, where Nefertiti would be treated with appropriate respect. Any surprise came from the fact that the outrage centred less on the fact that the experiment may have put a priceless antiquity in physical jeopardy, and more on the fact that the display of Nefertiti's 'naked' body was considered disrespectful. Mohammed al-Orabi, Egyptian ambassador to Germany, summed up the feelings of many of his outraged countrymen when he stated that the installation 'contradicts Egyptian manners and traditions. The body is almost naked, and Egyptian civilisation never displays a woman naked.'[23]

Can we learn anything practical from the Little Warsaw installation? We know that the Egyptians were making copper statues as early as the Second Dynasty reign of Khasekhemwy (c.2686 BCE), with the first surviving metal statues dating to the Sixth Dynasty reign of Pepi I (c.2321 BCE).[24] Little Warsaw's work leaves open the possibility that Nefertiti's bust may have been intended as part of a composite, mixed-material sculpture. But with no parallels, and absolutely no evidence to support this possibility, it seems highly unlikely.

If not part of a composite statue, could the bust have been a teaching aid? Nefertiti's missing left eye could then be explained as a demonstration which was halted before it was complete. The idea of a dedicated teaching aid leaves us with the curious and in many ways unsatisfactory image of Thutmose's students watching, passive, as he teaches his skills in a classroom situation. In reality, it seems highly unlikely that anyone would waste precious time and resources in this way; in Egypt, apprentices learned on the job. More credible is the suggestion that the bust was an artist's model or template, used to guide Thutmose's workers. This fits well with what we know of established working practices; the artists who decorated Egypt's tomb and temple walls, for example, routinely worked from patterns and guides which ensured the consistency of their work. By providing his workers with an approved image to copy, Thutmose could be confident that all his Nefertitis would look alike, and that all would be acceptable to the king.[25]

We can push this speculation further. We know that the Amarna elite were expected to perform their personal devotions before carved statues or stelae depicting the king and queen. We also know that Thutmose, by virtue of his role as the creator of the royal image, was in constant contact with the palace administration. His ownership of a chariot suggests that he may even have been one of the favoured few who accompanied the royal family as they processed along the royal road, presenting themselves to their admiring subjects. He must surely have had his own, conspicuous, royal icons. Could the Akhenaten and Nefertiti busts – which may indeed have served as models for the workforce – have been Thutmose's personal devotional aids? This would have been unusual, but Thutmose was an atypical man living in extraordinary times, and he had access to resources that others lacked.

Although there is no precedent for royal busts being used as cult objects in private contexts during the Eighteenth Dynasty, private busts were not unknown at this time. Approximately 150 so-called 'ancestor busts' have been discovered at sites throughout Egypt, with the majority coming from the Theban workmen's village of Deir el-Medina, and just one coming from Amarna. They range in date from the earlier Eighteenth Dynasty to the Nineteenth. These, our final example of deliberately manufactured disembodied heads, are images of (we assume) deceased family members. The majority take the form of a head approximately 25cm (10in) in height, with or without a wig, set on a base. Several double busts are known; these invariably show one head wearing a wig and one without. It is difficult to be specific about gender, but it is probable that the majority of the busts are female. Most of the busts are made from limestone, but there are also examples made from sandstone, granite, wood and clay. While many still bear traces of their original paint, only four are inscribed. The ancestor busts do not resemble living people in the way that the Nefertiti and Akhenaten busts do; instead, they resemble the upper part of an anthropoid coffin. It is generally accepted that they were designed to be set into niches in the village houses and tombs, where they served as the focal point for ancestor worship.[26]

Beneath the Skin

The addition of the fine layer of gypsum plaster to the limestone core allowed the artist to create the fine definition of muscles and tendons obvious in Nefertiti's neck, to add subtle creases around her mouth and under the eyes, and to emphasise her cheekbones. This turned Nefertiti from an unrealistically smooth being into a mature woman with considerable allure. These humanising creases and wrinkles were not, however, obvious to early visitors who, forced to view the queen under the strong, direct light provided by the museum, saw the brash and flattened appearance identifiable in many early photographs. To some, this idealised face with its heavy eyeliner, groomed black brows and defined red lips looked excessively made-up rather than elegant. Ironically, the replica busts which could be purchased from the museum and displayed at home under less harsh conditions, in many ways appeared more 'real' than the original.

Then, in 2001, when the bust was being moved within the Egyptian Museum in Berlin-Charlottenburg, it accidentally stood for a time in semi-darkness after a spotlight failed. This prompted the museum staff to start experimenting, and they quickly discovered that lighting the bust obliquely from behind increased Nefertiti's apparent age by approximately ten years. The muscles and tendons in her neck, the lines running from her nose to the mouth, the indentations at the side of her mouth, the wrinkles under her eyes and her slightly hollowed cheeks were all emphasised. In the words of Dietrich Wildung, who as Director of the Egyptian Museum and Papyrus Collection in Berlin had more opportunity than most to gaze at Nefertiti's face: 'the pretty model became a beautiful woman, aged by some years and more attractive than ever before'.[27] This more mature Nefertiti is the version of the bust that the museum now strives to present to its visitors.

In 1992 the bust was scanned using computed tomography (CT). This revealed that, while most of the bust was made from stone covered by a layer of plaster only a millimetre or two thick, the shoulders and the back part of the crown had essentially been created from plaster. In 2006, with more advanced technologies available, the bust was rescanned.[28] It was now possible to see how the plaster layer had been moulded to correct or personalise the well-made but somewhat generic stone head beneath, so that, for example, a slight bump on the stone nose was smoothed out to give a straight profile. The restoration work done to the crown and shoulders by the ancient craftsmen was apparent, as was more modern restoration performed between 1980 and 1984 on the thorax. These results are of great importance as they allow the museum's conservators to understand which areas of the bust are the most delicate, and the most susceptible to damage.

The Nefertiti scans were released to the general public, and received good coverage in the world's press, who seized on the 'fact' that Nefertiti apparently had a hidden face covered in irregularities. As Bernhard Illerhaus and his colleagues noted after analysing and discussing the data generated by the two Nefertiti CT scans, a calculated CT image cannot be regarded as a portrait. Nevertheless, headlines such as 'Beauty of the Nile Unmasked: Wrinkles and All' and 'Nefertiti's Real, Wrinkled Face Found in Famous Bust?' proliferated, and soon after came the acceptance that the addition of the smooth outer layer was the 'ancient-day version of photo-shopping'.[29] The face beneath the plaster must have been hidden on the queen's orders because it was too realistic, too wrinkled and, basically, too old to be seen. This is, of course, a huge assumption. The twenty-first-century press may believe that older women should be ashamed of their appearance, but we have no evidence to suggest that the ancient Egyptians felt the same way. In a land where few grew old, old age was not automatically linked to decay and death, and the wisdom of age is more likely to have been admired than denied.[30] If we take a close look at the stone and plaster heads recovered from the Thutmose workshop we see a lifelike combination of eye bags, nasolabial folds (the crease running along the edge of the cheek, connecting the corner of the nose to the mouth) and lines at the corners of the mouth. Even the princesses, who by no one's definition can be considered old, have lines at the corners of the mouth.

We don't know how old Nefertiti was when her bust was created. The face shows none of the unnatural angularity of earlier Amarna sculpture, and on this basis alone we can tentatively date it to Akhenaten's regnal year 12, or later. We know that by this point in Akhenaten's reign Nefertiti had already given birth to the six full-term children who are depicted in a dated scene in the Amarna tomb of Meryre II; she could, of course, have had other children (boys?) and failed pregnancies. While she could in theory have been less than twenty years old, it seems reasonable to assume that she was several years older, though not many decades older as her youngest daughter, Setepenre, was still a baby. Whatever her age, it is unlikely that she had the smooth albeit slightly wrinkled complexion of the Berlin bust. Nefertiti's life was more pampered than many, but she could not have avoided illnesses and minor accidents that would have marked her skin and, given the lack of dental hygiene combined with the elite liking for breads flavoured with honey, we may speculate that her teeth were not in good condition either.

Of relevance here is a small unfinished limestone statuette of Nefertiti, just 40cm (16in) tall, discovered in fragments in Thutmose's pantry.[31] This version of the queen has facial grooves and a downturned mouth which make her look tired or old, although it is entirely possible that the sculptor would have added a layer of painted plaster which would have given her a smoother and more youthful face. Nefertiti wears the cap crown and rounded earrings, leaving us with the faint possibility that this may be Kiya, although the cap crown and square-jawed face strongly suggest Nefertiti. She stands straight with her hands by her side, and her unpleated linen dress clings tightly to her body, giving the impression that she is naked. There are signs that her shoulders would have been covered by a linen shawl; she wears thonged sandals on her feet. Through the dress we see that her hips are wide, her stomach rounded, her breasts small and 'slack'.[32] She has the body of a woman who has borne children. There is no reason to assume that Nefertiti was ashamed of this body and, indeed, it would appear that neither Nefertiti nor Tiy was afraid of being presented as an older, experienced woman; the equivalent to the plump elder statesmen who occasionally appear in Egyptian art.

It is therefore unfortunate that the image of the smooth and slightly artificial Nefertiti is the one that persists in the public imagination. It is this image which has led to the modern association of Nefertiti with plastic surgery; there are Nefertiti clinics throughout the Western world, while the 'Nefertiti face lift' is promoted as a lower face, non-surgical option for those who might wish to 'tighten up sagging and wrinkled skin while erasing a few years'.[33] Even more unfortunate, perhaps, are the more than fifty surgical procedures (including eight nose jobs, three chin implants and three facelifts) which have transformed a British woman, Nileen Namita, into a living version of the Berlin bust, at a conservative cost of £200,000. Nileen believes that she is a reincarnation of Nefertiti: 'being Nefertiti is my destiny … Suffering is part of being Nefertiti. She suffered too, under the pressure of being queen.'[34]

Nileen is an extreme example of women who choose to associate with Nefertiti through their skin. Others, less extreme, create a connection with the bust, and through the bust with Nefertiti herself, via jewellery or skin art. Egyptology student Robin Snell explained to me the very personal relationship that can exist between a modern American woman and a long-dead Egyptian queen:

My Nefertiti tattoo is large, six inches long and five and a half inches wide. Its placement is at a place where it cannot be easily hidden. I want it to be seen. My tattoo artist knows I take them very serious so she actually studied Nefertiti before starting the piece.

When I lived in the San Francisco Bay Area I ran a very large domestic violence agency for battered women and children. As a director of intervention services, I worked with staff and clients in the role of a powerful woman who walked the walk and talked the talk. I worked with my partners and my husband, and raised and loved my son. That's my mirroring with Nefertiti. She ruled with her husband, sometimes ruled alone and loved her children. Many around the world think she's the perfect beauty but looking at her closely, the eye is gone, pieces of the ear broken off, very important to me. We must look at each other deeper to see the strength. Behind her, we put a sunset/sunrise to acknowledge Nefertiti will always be in front, supported forever by Ra with the outline of a falcon on top of an ankh ... Nefertiti and I should wear a T-shirt that states, 'Well-behaved women rarely make history.'[35]

The Colourful Queen

Occasionally, museums will display replica sculptures painted with authentic pigments so that they appear to a modern audience as they would have appeared to their ancient creators. This always comes as a shock: the colourful sculptures look totally different from what we have come to regard as the original, clean stone versions; garish, unsubtle and, in many ways, less authentic.[36] The Nefertiti bust can provoke a similar response, although in this case the paint-work is genuinely old. We have become so accustomed to seeing Egyptian sculpture unpainted, its hidden stone exposed, that the colourful queen can appear unacceptably modern and un-Egyptian to our preconditioned eyes. We forget that most Egyptian sculpture in the round, relief sculpture and painting was completed in full colour. The mineral-based paint was applied in solid blocks or, occasionally, in patterns, shading was rare, and the overall effect was far from subtle.[37] Where traces of ancient paint do survive on a statue they may not adequately convey the vivid nature of the original, because Egyptian pigments are not entirely stable, and may deteriorate and lose intensity over time.

We have already watched Iuty paint Princess Baketaten. We can see another painter at work in the near-contemporary Theban tomb of Rekhmire. Rekhmire, vizier to the earlier Eighteenth Dynasty king Tuthmosis III (c.1479–1425 BCE), decorated his tomb with images of his daily responsibilities, which included control of the royal sculpture workshops. In one scene we can see artisans rubbing rounded stones over the surfaces of stone statues to smooth and polish them, while other workers add the finishing touches and

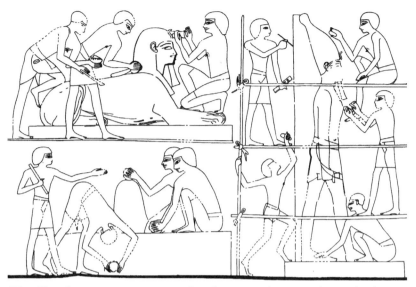

New Kingdom artists creating royal sculpture, as shown in the tomb of Rekhmire (TT 100). After Davies 1943, Plate LX

identifying inscriptions to the royal images using paintbrushes and pens.[38] This fits well with what we understand of the finishing process, which might include the addition of eyes inlaid with white and black stone bound by a copper line. A soft stone statue might be smoothed, plastered and painted in bright, mineral-based colours, while a hard stone statue might be polished and, perhaps, partially painted or gilded to pick out elements such as clothing and regalia, while the king's flesh was left as polished stone. It was unusual for a hard stone statue to be entirely covered in plaster and paint (the plaster being necessary for the paint to stick), as the colour of the stone itself had symbolic importance. Quartzite and red granite, for example, had strong solar connections; this may explain why Akhenaten favoured yellow-red and purple quartzite for his Amarna statues. At Amarna, quartzite was almost entirely used for female statues, although Akhenaten did have quartzite shabti figures. Today Amarna is a place of mud-brick and sand; it is difficult to reconcile it with Akhenaten's glittering, colourful city decorated with stone, faience and glass-paste inlays, painted and gilded.

Tradition dictated that Egyptian men would be painted with a red-brown skin while their female relations would be given a yellow-white skin. This was neither a value judgement nor a reflection of daily life; it was simply a means of allowing the viewer to make an easy distinction between males and females of all ages. It was, however, a convention rather than a rule, and an Amarna woman might have a red-brown skin. The Berlin bust, which has a pinkish-brown skin tone, therefore tells us nothing about Nefertiti's actual skin colour. Ancient Egypt, a north-east African country with a Mediterranean border and a physical connection to the Near East, was filled, as Egypt is today, with African people of varying hue with, as a very general rule, skin being lighter in the north and darker in the south. Yet, swayed by the bust, many Western observers have unthinkingly assumed that Nefertiti was 'white', while many Afrocentrists have assumed that she was 'black', as they believe everyone in ancient Egypt to have been black. Some have assumed that the bust is a crude modern fake because it has the 'wrong' skin colour.[39] The ancient Egyptians themselves would not have understood this modern obsession with classifying people by skin colour and racial heritage: they divided their world into Egyptians (those who followed Egyptian customs and accepted Egyptian beliefs) and non-Egyptians (those who did not). Skin colour was utterly irrelevant to them; behaviour was what mattered.

This identification of Nefertiti as 'white' allowed Western women to identify with her. She was a popular subject at fancy-dress parties and in fashion-oriented journals which, throughout the 1920s and 30s, posted regular features comparing conventional Western beauties (none of whom were dark-skinned, bald or lacking an eye) to the bust. Some of these women aspired to look like Nefertiti by employing Egyptian-style makeup and costumes; others were simply photographed in profile with their hair swept back. Unusually, the *Sketch* of 21 January 1928 was happy to acknowledge a black Nefertiti. An article entitled 'The Black Journey', an exploration of the characters encountered on a trip across Africa, included 'A Negroid Nefertiti', a woman whose 'cast of feature and style of coiffure – Negroid as both undoubtedly are – are nevertheless reminiscent of the Egyptian queen who is now ranked as one of the world's immortal beauties'. The suggestion here is that the African beauty is like Nefertiti despite her black skin rather than because of it.

It is skin colour, rather than hairstyle, that allows us to differentiate between Egyptian images of boys and girls, both of whom have shaven heads. As these bald children grow up they assume gender specific hairstyles, with men cutting their hair short (though they might then cover their head with a wig) and women either cutting their hair to cover it with a wig, or growing it long. Nefertiti's bust lacks hair; it seems that the queen has either shaved her head or she has tucked her long hair up, inside her crown.[40] Her apparently bald head matches those of her daughters, whose elongated shaven heads usually feature the 'sidelock of youth'; a plait or series of plaits worn by elite children on the right side of the head, but whose quartzite heads recovered from the Thutmose villa are hairless. Where her hair is shown, Nefertiti favours the 'Nubian wig', a bushy, layered bob cut at an angle leaving the nape of the neck exposed. This style, which is believed to have been inspired by the naturally curly hair of the Nubian soldiers who fought in the Egyptian army, had previously been reserved for men connected with the military or the police force.[41] At Amarna it was adopted by both Nefertiti and Kiya.

Her lack of hair gives the Berlin Nefertiti a sleek, modern androgyny which is emphasised by the hint of an Adam's apple caused by the forward thrust of the neck and chin. Many find this attractive, but some find it unsettling. Camille Paglia, for example, suggests that

> *the bust of Nefertiti is artistically and ritualistically complete, exalted, harsh and alien ... This is the least consoling of great art works. Its popularity is based on misunderstanding and suppression of its unique features. The proper response to the Nefertiti bust is fear.*[42]

Kevin McGuiness attributes the bust's fascination to its mixture of male and female traits:

> *The enduring fame of the bust can be directly traced to the liminal sexuality of the Queen. The long nose, square jaw line and strong chin contribute to a striking portrait of a woman who processes directly masculine characteristics. The Queen's likeness operates between the dichotomous realms of the masculine and feminine, merging features associated with both sexes and creating a hybrid face which is at once captivating and unsettling.*[43]

It is difficult to equate this austere, androgynous queen with the Nefertiti admired by James Baikie:

> *The portraits of other queens of romance, such as Cleopatra and Mary of Scotland, are apt to leave one wondering where the charm came in about which all men raved; but no one could question for a moment the beauty of Nefertiti. Features of exquisite modelling and delicacy, the long graceful neck of an Italian princess of the Renaissance, and an expression of gentleness not untouched with melancholy, make up the presentation of a royal lady about whom we should like to know a great deal, and actually know almost nothing.*[44]

Clearly, beauty is a subjective issue; a personal feeling. And yet the Nefertiti bust is almost universally acknowledged to be the portrait of a beautiful woman. Despite the evidence of the awkward, angular Nefertiti carved on the Theban temple walls, and the older, tired Nefertiti created in Thutmose's workshop, we are happy to accept the bust as the one true likeness of the queen, and to draw the inevitable unscientific conclusion: 'Pharaoh's principal wife, Nefertiti, was one of the most beautiful women of her generation.'[45]

Why is the Berlin Nefertiti so beautiful to so many us, irrespective of age, gender, race or culture? It may be that we find her beautiful simply because we expect to find her beautiful; she has, after all, been promoted as one of the world's most beautiful women for almost a century, and she now has a very familiar face. Her romantic back-story, too, makes her very attractive: many of us are fascinated by the cloud of wealth, power and religious mystery that obscures the Amarna court. David Perrett's studies of facial perception suggest another reason.[46] Many of us find very symmetrical faces attractive, and the Berlin Nefertiti has a strikingly symmetrical face. Only her ears appear asymmetrical, with the left being more rounded at the lobe than the pointed right. This is likely to be either the result of damage sustained in antiquity or, as the recent CT scans suggest, the result of flint inclusions within the limestone core causing the sculptors to vary their work slightly.[47]

Using a grid superimposed on a photogrammetric image of the frontal view of the Nefertiti bust, Rolf Krauss has demonstrated that the sculptor used a grid to calculate the proportions of the bust, employing the 'fingerbreadth', the smallest measurement of length used by the Egyptians (1.875cm; 0.74in), as the base unit.[48] Everything can be measured in fingerbreadths so that, for example, the crown is nine fingerbreadths tall above the queen's forehead, and measures thirteen fingerbreadths at its widest point. The mouth is one fingerbreadth tall, the ear three fingerbreadths, and the distance between the eyebrows one fingerbreadth. Some find this symmetry off-putting; Nefertiti may be technically beautiful, but she is remote and artificial. To Borchardt, who scrupulously avoids using the word 'beautiful', this symmetry endows Nefertiti with an aura of peace, making her

> *the epitome of tranquillity and harmony. Viewed straight on it is perfectly symmetrical, but nevertheless, the viewer is never in doubt that he has before him not just any imaginary ideal image but rather the likeness, at once stylised but simultaneously true, of a specific person with a highly distinctive appearance.*[49]

If Borchardt is correct, and the bust is true to life, Nefertiti's symmetry is unusual. Most of us have one more expressive (and therefore more wrinkled) side, and our faces often exhibit variations in nostril size, ear shape and mouth curvature. We might expect to find the same symmetry, and the same measurements between features, apparent in the other heads identified as Nefertiti; however, this is not the case. While all the carved heads identified as Nefertiti share similarities – particularly with regard to the chin, mouth and cheekbones – they are not identical.

The fact that Nefertiti's 'flawless' beauty includes one very obvious flaw – a missing left eye – seems not to matter. This is less a sign of our modern tolerance of disability or differentness, and more a question of our ability to ignore what is before our own two eyes. Photographs are taken in profile with the empty socket hidden, replicas are created with the missing eye replaced, and many commentators simply ignore the problem, so that some visitors are taken aback when they come face to face with the real bust. My own ever-increasing collection of miniature Nefertiti busts, all acquired from gift shops within museums that have little or no obvious connection to Nefertiti, includes just one example where the left eye is still missing. All the others have been 'restored' to present a more conventional appearance.

Nefertiti's head extends forward from her neck, her chin slightly raised so that she looks visitors firmly in the eye. Wildung suggests that her gaze is 'directed energetically toward the front, fixed so directly on an invisible person opposite that is [sic] seems impossible to escape'. Of course, the impression that we have of Nefertiti as she sits on her museum plinth depends very much on our own height; we all get a slightly different view and we cannot all look her in the eye.[50] Her two eye sockets are roughly symmetrical, with an average depth of 3mm. The right eye is created from a ball of black-coloured wax placed in the white-painted eye-socket and covered with a thin (2mm) lens of rock-crystal engraved with the outline of the iris. The left eye contained no lens and no pupil. Both eyes are rimmed with black kohl, or eyeliner. When we notice the missing left eye, we tend to assume that the inlay has simply dropped out and been lost. Borchardt, for one, thought that this is what had happened. He tells us that, when it was recovered, the bust:

> *was almost complete. Parts of the ears were missing, and there was no inlay in the left eye. The dirt was searched and in part sieved. Some pieces of the ears were found, but not the eye inlay. Much later I realised that there had never been an inlay.*[51]

A substantial reward was offered for the recovery of the missing eye, but it had vanished without a trace. The partial sieving of the debris yielded a few ear fragments, and nothing else. It is perhaps unlikely that a thin crystal lens and a small ball of black wax would ever have been found by workmen who failed to find the far larger and more substantial uraeus, but its absence has led to suggestions that it was never present. An examination of the socket has proved inconclusive here; while there is no obvious trace of glue, scratch marks on the lower lid could have been caused when the inlay was inserted.[52]

We have already met, and discarded, the theory that the bust was a teaching aid. More fanciful explanations for the missing eye – for example, the suggestion that Thutmose deliberately wrenched the eye from the finished bust as a means of gaining revenge on the beautiful queen who had spurned him as a lover – lack both credibility and supporting evidence.[53] The explanation favoured by Arthur Weigall, that the bust is true to life, does not explain why her other images all show two apparently healthy eyes. In a newspaper article bluntly entitled 'The Beautiful, One-Eyed Nefertiti', Weigall told his readers that she had 'suffered the very common Egyptian misfortune of losing the sight of one of her eyes, over which a cataract had formed'.[54] The revelation of her 'defect', although contrary to established artistic tradition which would avoid any hint of deformity in a queen, was therefore yet another expression of the *maat*, or truth, favoured by the king. It could even be stated that, 'the triumph of Nefertiti's loveliness is enhanced by her deformity'.[55] This was certainly the belief of the Nefertiti Club, which was founded in the 1930s by 'the young wife of a prominent businessman in Omaha, Nebraska, who has a defect in her right eye':

Though most of the members are good looking, they all possess a defect in one of their eyes. But all like Nefertiti refuse to believe that their disability makes them less attractive, and as they go about their daily tasks none of them shows any signs of self-consciousness or embarrassment.[56]

PART II

RECREATING NEFERTITI

*Great interest has been aroused in archaeological circles over
the suggestion by the Egyptian government that the famous
bust of Nefertiti should returned to Egypt from the Museum
of Egyptology in Berlin. The bust was, apparently, taken out
of Egypt at the time when Herr Borchardt was excavating in
1914 on behalf of the German Archaeological Institute, the
site of Akhenaten's city at tel-el-Amarna. For some years this
bust remained quietly in Berlin, and it was not until the
early part of 1923 that its presence there became generally
known ... At once the bust was appreciated as one of the most
superb examples of the sculptor's art known to man, and replicas of it have by now permeated the civilised world. A few
weeks ago the German government agreed to receive commis-
sioners from Egypt to discuss the question of the ownership of
this bust, and the matter is under discussion at the moment ...
The legal aspect of the case will depend on the terms upon
which the German Institute were permitted to dig in Egyptian soil.*

The Sphere, 4 February 1928

5

THE COLOURFUL QUEEN

*As archaeologists and anthropologists we are arch-appropri-
ators of material culture. The objects we collect from ethno-
graphic contexts, the artefacts we find in the earth, are no
longer a part of the material culture to which they once
belonged. From the moment of collection or discovery they
become part of our material culture, our systems of cultural
significance.*[1]

Matt Edgeworth (2007)

By the turn of the twentieth century the days when a non-Egyptian
archaeologist could arrive at an archaeological site in Egypt, dig it
up and take his finds home to dispose of as he wished, had long
gone. While Egypt was a British protectorate, veiled from 1882–1914
then *de facto* from 1914–56, the French-run Antiquities Service protected Egypt's heritage. No archaeological mission could excavate or
export antiquities without their permission. As we might expect,
relationships between the foreign excavators and the French officials

were not always as cordial as they could have been, and many of the excavators regarded the Antiquities Service – which they considered to be French rather than Egyptian – as acting in direct conflict to the interests of Egyptology.

In 1907 the eminent Egyptologist Gaston Maspero was both Director of the Antiquities Service and head of the Egyptian Museum in Cairo. He awarded the concession to dig at Amarna to the German entrepreneur and philanthropist James Simon – a man who, thanks to his co-ownership of the largest cotton wholesale firm in Europe, could count himself one of the ten richest in Prussia.[2] Simon shared his good fortune generously, allocating up to a third of his personal income to building public baths and homes for disadvantaged children, financing concerts and public lectures, stocking Berlin's newly opened National Gallery and eventually, in 1898, founding the German Oriental Society (Deutsche Orient-Gesellschaft, or DOG). His philanthropy led to his inclusion in the regular 'gentlemen's evenings' held by Kaiser Wilhelm II. They developed a friendship despite the fact that Simon was Jewish while the Kaiser was prone to anti-Semitism. It may be that they were united by their shared passion for archaeology. Simon, who was the treasurer of the DOG, funded the Amarna excavations with lavish donations from his own pocket while Wilhelm, who took over the role of patron of the DOG in 1901, financed excavations with awards from imperial funds.

Simon would not personally excavate at Amarna; the work was to be done by a team of archaeologists from the DOG, supervised by Ludwig Borchardt. However, by paying for the excavation directly, rather than donating the money to the DOG and allowing them to make the payments, Simon enabled the society to avoid the hefty donation tax that would have reduced the value of his contribution significantly. It has been estimated that the excavations cost him approximately 30,000 Goldmark each season.[3] As was common on archaeological digs at this time, Borchardt would not be continually present at Amarna, but would delegate many of his responsibilities to a junior colleague, Hermann Ranke. The actual digging – the manual labour – would be done not by the Europeans but by a team of experienced locals.

Ludwig Borchardt was also, by 1907, an eminent Egyptologist. Born in 1863 in Berlin, he had studied architecture before turning to Egyptology and becoming a pupil of the distinguished linguist Adolf Erman. In 1895 he joined the Department of Egyptian Art in the Berlin Museum, and paid his first visit to Egypt. From 1896–9, as an employee of the Egyptian Antiquities Service, he worked alongside Maspero to produce the *Catalogue Général* of the Cairo Museum. Colleagues they may have been, but Borchardt and Maspero were never good friends, and their private correspondence shows that each was critical of the other.[4] Having excavated some of Egypt's Fifth Dynasty pyramids and sun temples, in 1907 Borchardt became the founding director of the German Archaeological Institute (Deutsches Archëologisches Institut, or DAI) in Cairo. He was to excavate at Amarna until the outbreak of the Great War caused him to return to Germany.

The Beautiful Woman Arrives

Work at Amarna started with a survey of the city, and the cutting of an exploratory series of trenches that would indicate where the richest archaeological rewards lay hidden. This investigative phase was followed by excavation proper. Starting in the eastern section of the city the team dug their way along High Priest Street in what today we would consider a rather random fashion. On 6 December 1912, digging in the remains of Thutmose's villa, they found a collection of stone and plaster pieces lying in Room 19. Happily,

Borchardt was on site that day, and able to observe the excavation in progress. Ten years after the event, he published an account of the find:

> *After my lunch break on December 6, 1912, I found a note by Prof. Ranke who was the supervisor, in which he asked me to come to House 47.2 ... I went there and saw the pieces of Amenophis IV's life-sized bust, which had just been discovered right behind the door in room 19. Soon after and close to the same place in room 19, very delicate and fragile pieces were found. It seemed wise to call the most diligent worker, Mohammed Ahmed es-Snussi, and let him do the work alone, and order one of the younger men to record the work in writing. Slowly but surely we worked our way through the debris, which was only about 1.10 m. high, towards the east wall of room 19 ... About 0.2 m. from the east wall and 0.35 m. from the north wall, on a level with our knees, a flesh colored neck with painted red straps appeared. 'Life-size colorful bust of Queen' was recorded. The tools were put aside, and the hands were now used. The following minutes confirmed what appeared to be a bust: above the neck, the lower part of the bust was uncovered, and underneath it, the back part of the Queen's wig appeared. It took a considerable amount of time until the whole piece was completely freed from all the dirt and rubble. This was due to the fact that a portrait head of the king, which lay close to the bust, had to be recovered first.*[5]

His official excavation diary, written on the day of the discovery, gives a concise description of the colourful queen and includes a small sketch of the bust:

> *Life-sized painted bust of the queen, 47cm high. With the blue wig cut straight on top, and garlanded by a ribbon half-way up.*

Colours look freshly painted. Really wonderful work. No use describing it, you have to see it.[6]

Less helpful his rather cryptic reflection on the discovery:

Were I to describe this discovery here as it really took place, with its confusion, its surprises, its hopes and also its minor disappointments, the reader would certainly be as confused thereby as we were at the time, when we made notes in the studio, and had hardly got the particulars of one find to paper before two further objects to be measured and noted were uncovered.[7]

A preliminary report and photographs were sent to Berlin, where they greatly excited the directors of the DOG. It was hoped that the bust would be allowed to travel to Germany, but this would be entirely dependent on the goodwill of the Antiquities Service. There was nothing that the DOG could do to influence the decision.

In 1912 all non-Egyptian holders of excavation licences were entitled to a share of each season's finds. This division, or *partage*, was designed to protect Egypt's heritage by ensuring that no unique items and no items of great archaeological or commercial value left Egypt, while allowing those who financed excavations a tangible reward for their generosity. As a result, a stream of legally acquired and properly documented antiquities flowed out of Egypt and into private and public collections in Europe and America. Today the division of finds is generally seen as a bad thing: it breaks up groups of interrelated artefacts, turns a scientific excavation into a treasure hunt and encourages excavators to discard what they may perceive as insignificant discoveries in order to ensure that their share of finds is not entirely comprised of broken potsherds. The assumption that the proper place for an Egyptian artefact is a foreign museum smacks of colonialism and what cultural critic Edward W. Said has defined as the 'manipulation or management of native societies for imperial purposes'.[8]

A century ago, opinions were very different. Western archaeologists regarded their digs as a legitimate means of exploring mysteries of the past – in many cases they were interested in exploring the truth of the history expressed in the Bible – which brought employment to some of the poorest areas of Egypt while stimulating the tourism that brought money to the country as a whole. But with little or no institutional funding available, all archaeological missions were dependent on sponsors, and those sponsors liked to be rewarded for their generosity. The end-of-dig division was therefore a necessary means of financing work that benefited everyone, while sharing out the trophies of mankind's shared past. The acquisition of artefacts was particularly important to the DOG, who were keen to collect archaeological finds from across the Near East to create a museum for Berlin which could rival the far older collections housed in the British Museum in London and the Louvre in Paris. When, within a few years of Borchardt's discovery, Egyptian law was changed to end the 50:50 division of finds and prevent private individuals such as Simon from holding concessions and so acquiring artefacts, many gloomily prophesied the end of all fieldwork in Egypt. Flinders Petrie, a former Amarna excavator, summed up the feelings of many when he said that 'the Egyptian government is taking everything but is not paying the cost of excavation which terms are impossible'.[9] For him at least, the outcome was inevitable, and Petrie abandoned a lifetime's work in Egypt to excavate in Palestine. It is worth reading his views on this subject at some length, as they demonstrate the attitudes of the time very clearly:

The issue of new and arbitrary conditions by Lacau [Pierre Lacau, Maspero's replacement as head of the Antiquities Service] was a repetition of what former French Directors of Antiquities had tried to do. This attempt had been checked before ... by the strength of the British management. Now that Britain was leaving much more to Egyptian direction, there was not the same check, and French autocracy was uncontrolled ... The applicant was required to renounce all rights to any share of his discoveries, to send in the names of his workmen to be sanctioned, never to see his friends without a permit from the government, and not to put up any shelters or structure without submitting plans to be approved. In this condition of affairs there was a general reluctance to continue work.[10]

Not everyone, of course, agreed with Petrie. The American Egyptologist and fieldworker James Henry Breasted, for one, regarded Petrie as little more than a spade for hire; a 'mere digger after museum pieces and stuff to satisfy his subscribers'.[11] But many older Egyptologists did think that the new rules were unfair; Egyptology was about to end, and the French were not to be trusted.

The seemingly insatiable Western interest in ancient Egypt had led, in many cases, to a desire to actually own parts of ancient Egypt. Growing numbers of tourists were sailing down the Nile before returning home laden with mummies, shabtis and papyri, at least some of which were genuine. Armchair Egyptologists were acquiring large and important (and often looted) collections from dealers, while some 'respectable' museum curators were not averse to enhancing their collections with antiquities purchased on the black market. The sites and monuments were under ever increasing threat as everyone, it seemed, wanted a genuinely ancient souvenir. Recognising that something had to be done, Maspero had, in 1899, managed to acquire enough funding to appoint two antiquities inspectors, whom he charged with protecting the archaeological sites. One was to be based in Cairo with responsibility for all the northern sites, while the other was to live in Luxor and supervise all the southern sites. The inspectors were required to ensure that the sites and monuments were properly excavated, properly conserved and properly guarded; any thefts or acts of vandalism had to be investigated and resolved. In 1904 a third post was created, with Maspero's protégé Gustave Lefebvre being named Antiquities Inspector for Middle Egypt, an area that included Amarna. Lefebvre was a papyrologist with an interest in ancient language rather than Eighteenth Dynasty art and architecture, but this was not considered a problem; the three antiquities inspectors, burdened with what today seems as an impossibly huge workload, were not accorded the luxury of specialisation.

On 15 January 1913 the *Aegyptische Nachrichten*, a weekly newsletter for German ex-pats, carried an article describing the marvellous discoveries at Amarna, which apparently included 'a room that was filled from top to bottom with unfinished sculptures, heads of kings and queens'.[12] This would have worried Borchardt: as an excavator, he would naturally have wanted to keep the best finds for his sponsor, and unauthorised and exaggerated public recognition of his discoveries immediately before the division would not have helped his cause. On 16 January 1913 he wrote to Lefebvre, asking for a 'speedy division of finds', possibly hoping that Lefebvre had not yet seen the article. The division was subsequently fixed for 20 January 1913, with Maspero's approval.

Bruno Güterbock, secretary of the DOG and editor of its newsletter, was a guest in the Amarna excavation house at the time of the division. A decade after the event, soon after the Nefertiti bust had been revealed to the public in Berlin, he wrote a 'strictly confidential' explanation of division day to Günther Roeder, director of Hildersheim's Roemer-Pelizaeus Museum and board member of the DOG. Included with his letter was a copy of the signed division protocol; the official document which gave Simon title to specified finds. Güterbock was able to describe the growing apprehension amongst the excavation team members as the inspector's visit approached:

> *You can imagine that we all had very little hope that this wonderful piece would not go to Cairo, so little, that on the evening before Lefebvre's arrival, all the inhabitants of the excavation house walked in solemn procession, candle in hand, to the storeroom to bid our farewell – we did not expect anything else – to the 'coloured queen'. Later, though, Borchardt negotiated in such a clever way that she fell to the German side.*[13]

A brand-new Antiquities Law (Number 14, dated 12 June 1912; effective as of 1 July 1912) was designed to clarify and consolidate all previous laws relating to the ownership, sale and export of antiquities. All antiquities were to be regarded as the property of the state, and an export licence could only be granted by the Antiquities Service. Article 12 stipulated that 'finds from an excavation shall be divided by partition into two shares of equal value in the same manner provided by Article 11 of the law'. Article 11, which dealt with a division between the state and an individual who had made a legal find, outlined more precisely how the division should be made. Crucially, however the finds were divided, the Antiquities Service had a right of pre-emption which allowed them to acquire any find, no matter where in the division it had been allocated.[14] The 'two shares of equal value' stipulation was aimed as much at Maspero as at the excavators under his control. The government felt that he had been unduly lenient in allocating finds to foreign missions, while Maspero himself felt it important to encourage the foreign missions who were helping him to preserve Egypt's archaeological sites from the threat of settlement and agricultural expansion. Borchardt, wary of the new system, recorded his thoughts in his diary: 'We shall be the first victims of the new decree of the ministry of finances.'[15]

As the new law demanded, the Amarna finds were split into two lists. One list was headed by a small painted and inscribed stone stela; part of a household shrine showing Akhenaten, Nefertiti and their three eldest daughters sitting beneath the rays of the Aten. The other list was headed by the Nefertiti bust.[16] Lefebvre reached Amarna at noon and, as Güterbock tells us, the division started with the inspector examining photographs of the finds. He was then given access to both the excavation records and the finds themselves; these lay in open crates in the dimly lit storeroom. Although, as Güterbock later stressed, 'had he [Lefebvre] wished to do so, he could have taken out any individual object which he might have liked to examine more closely', Lefebvre made the most cursory of inspections, and declined the opportunity to physically handle the finds. It seemed to Güterbock that the inspector had already decided which share he was to take. The excavation diary paints the picture of a more conscientious Lefebvre:

> *Then he looked at the finds on the bureau; there the excavation journals were put at his disposal. With special care, he viewed the objects in hard stone: stela, the colourful queen, the statues and heads of the princesses, the queen and the king.*[17]

But, as Borchardt later confided to the art critic Julius Meier-Graefe, 'the gents in Cairo were just too slack to look in the box'.[18] From the diary we learn that the division was formally agreed and the protocol, which was written in French, signed that night after dinner. As Lefebvre did not claim the list headed by the bust, and declined to exercise his right of pre-emption to transfer the bust to his own share, ownership of the bust fell to Simon as the holder of the Amarna concession.

Borchardt left Amarna for Cairo on 23 January, taking the Nefertiti bust with him. On 5 February he wrote to Heinrich Schäfer at the Neues Museum in Berlin, informing him that the bust would soon be on its way:

> *Today H.M. [Her Majesty] shall leave my house where she was accommodated since Sunday. Thus you will see her soon after this letter turns up. I hope you enjoy it. I shall be calm only when I receive the telegram about her arrival.*[19]

In late February 1913 the Nefertiti bust arrived at Tiergartenstrasse 15a, Simon's Berlin home. A month later, the other Amarna finds reached the Neues Museum. With great generosity Maspero, who had not actually seen the 1912/13 finds, had agreed that they should all travel to Berlin for an exhibition; the Egyptian share would then return to Cairo. The exhibition opened on 5 November 1913, in the Egyptian Courtyard of the Neues Museum. As Maximilian Rapsiber, writing for the Berlin weekly journal *Der Roland von Berlin*, reported on 13 November 1913:

> *Curious visitors flocked in droves into the otherwise so deserted columned hall of the Berlin Egyptian Museum, only to be awestruck. First and foremost amongst them archaeologically inspired ladies and teenagers. Columns of youngsters, resplendent in colourful caps, push their way straight through the colourful throng of serious looking pedagogues. The buzz of sensation wafts between the papyrus capitals of the colourful temple hall. We admit; the scholars rummaging through the earth have not exaggerated this time: true works of art and curiosities of unprecedented attraction have surfaced here.*[20]

The exhibition was a great success. Initially scheduled for just a few weeks, it remained open well into the New Year, exposing the general public to the art and sculpture of the Amarna Period for the first time. Until this point, most assessments of Amarna art had been based on the tomb scenes published by Lepsius. Art historians Georges Perrot and Charles Chipiez had summed up the feelings of many when they described Akhenaten:

[W]e find nothing that can be compared to the almost fantastic personality of Amenophis, with his low, unintellectual forehead, his pendulous cheeks, his feminine contours and his general expression of gloom and melancholy. The fidelity with which these unpleasing features are reproduced is extraordinary and can only be accounted for by the existence of a tradition so well established that no one thought of breaking it.[21]

Now the public could see with their own eyes that, away from the tomb, Amarna art had a vibrant, modern appeal. The pieces recovered from Thutmose's workshop could have come from any contemporary art gallery. Furthermore the heads – the plaster heads – looked not like statues, but like the normal people who walked the streets of Berlin. The exhibition attracted great press attention, and members of the public flocked to the museum.[22] When the Egyptian-owned objects returned to Cairo in February 1914 they were replaced in the exhibition by plaster casts made in the museum's Gipsformerei, or plaster workshop. And the public continued to flock to the exhibition.

The public, however, did not see the Nefertiti bust. It had made a brief appearance at the opening of the exhibition, and had then been withdrawn at Borchardt's request. Güterbock confirms our suspicions: despite urging from the museum and the DOG, Borchardt was reluctant to display the Nefertiti head because he knew that the Antiquities Service was likely to be very unhappy that a masterpiece had slipped through their fingers, and an unhappy Antiquities Service might well terminate the DOG's concession to excavate at Amarna. This delay in display was ultimately to fuel speculation that the bust had a dubious provenance. In fact, there was an early publication of the bust. In October 1913 Borchardt published an illustrated article on the 1912/13 excavations which included images of the stone and plaster pieces recovered from Thutmose's workshop. This included a small black-and-white photograph of the Nefertiti bust displayed in right profile with the crown and shoulders cut off. There was no reaction to this first public appearance; it seems that no one noticed.[23]

For several weeks Nefertiti sat on Simon's desk, watching him as he worked. It was either here, or in a private viewing at the Neues Museum, that the Kaiser first inspected the bust. In October 1913 Simon presented Wilhelm with one of two replicas of the bust which he had commissioned from the young sculptor Tina Haim (later Tina Haim-Wentscher; subsequently Tina Haim-Wentcher). Haim already had experience of replicating ancient sculptures in the Berlin Museum. Her replica Nefertitis were not exact copies, they were made from artificial stone and they had been 'tidied up', with the uraeus, damaged ears and missing left eye restored. Nevertheless, the Kaiser was delighted with his gift, and wrote an effusive letter of thanks to Simon. His version of the Nefertiti bust would eventually accompany him into exile at Huis Doorn in the Netherlands, where it remains today. Simon kept the second replica for himself, displaying it in his living room underneath portraits of his parents.

The genuine bust was sent on loan to the Neues Museum on 20 October 1913. On 7 July 1920 Simon donated his entire Amarna collection to the museum, transferring ownership of the artefacts to the State of Prussia. The bust would undergo a final change of ownership in 1957 when, with the State of Prussia dissolved, title to all cultural assets owned prior to 1945 was transferred to the newly created Prussian Cultural Heritage Foundation (Stiftung Preussischer Kulturbesitz, or SPK). Today the SPK, Germany's largest cultural institution, controls Berlin's sixteen state-run museums plus the State Library and the Secret State Archive of Prussia. Conscious that there are legal and ethical questions over the ownership of many of the pieces in its collections, the SPK is working with countries of origin with the aim of preserving 'a shared heritage'.[24] This includes working with the Egyptian Ministry of Culture on the creation of an Akhenaten Museum in Minya, Middle Egypt, which will display the most recent finds from the site. Currently, the SPK remains the legal owner of the Nefertiti bust.

Simon's international business suffered during the Great War, and suffered again during the period of German hyperinflation that followed. Simon Brothers went bankrupt in 1929, with Simon auctioning the two most valuable pieces in his art collection – a Franz Hals and a Vermeer – to top up his employees' pension fund. A plaque acknowledging Simon's contribution to Egyptology was added to the Amarna Hall of the Neues Museum on the occasion of his eightieth birthday in 1931. Two years later, it would be removed by the Nazis. Simon died in relative poverty in 1932, and was buried in Berlin's Jewish cemetery. The Kaiser, exiled in the Netherlands, sent a wreath to his friend's funeral.

Following Adolf Hitler's rise to power and the corresponding increase in anti-Semitism, there was a deliberate attempt to expunge Simon's role as Berlin's most generous benefactor. As his family fled Berlin, his name was effectively erased from the public record. When the war ended Museum Island – a complex of separate museums which together formed one large complex dedicated to science and the arts, including the Neues Museum – was allocated to East Berlin. The communist East German authorities had little interest in reviving the memory of a bourgeois Jew, although a commemoration of his Amarna work was held in 1982. Recently, however, following German reunification, steps have been taken to restore Simon's memory. His story has been recorded in a television documentary,

1 a, b, c: The plastered and painted bust of a queen, identified by her crown as Nefertiti, wife of Akhenaten, recovered from the Amarna workshop of the chief of works Thutmose, and now displayed in the Neues Museum, Berlin.

2. Stela showing the Amarna royal family – Akhenaten, Nefertiti and their three eldest daughters – sitting beneath the rays of the Aten. The royal family take the place of the traditional gods who have been banished under Akhenaten's henotheistic regime.

3. A broken bust of Akhenaten, recovered from Thutmose's Amarna workshop.

4. An aging Nefertiti: statuette recovered from the Thutmose workshop.

5. The Sakkara tomb of the late Eighteenth Dynasty artist Thutmose. The door has been bricked up in modern times to protect the tomb.

6. Colossal head of 'Orus', Amenhotep III, wearing the double crown of Upper and Lower Egypt, recovered from Thebes.

7. Small wooden head of Queen Tiy, recovered from Gurob. The head and its crown, once part of a composite statue, have been extensively re-worked in antiquity.

8. Archaeologist Ludwig Borchardt (sitting) with visitors at Amarna, December 1912.

9. The painted and inscribed stela, part of a household shrine, chosen by Inspector Gustave Lefebvre in place of the Nefertiti bust.

10. The discovery of the 'life-sized colourful bust of queen' in the ruined Amarna workshop of the sculptor Thutmose, 6 December, 1912.

11 a, b, c, d, e: A modern Nefertiti emerges from a block of Portland limestone.

12. Little Warsaw's installation *The Body of Nefertiti:* a work which took as its inspiration the redisplay of popular and historical symbols in contemporary contexts. The ancient bust was for a brief time displayed on a modern metal body.

13. Fred Wilson's 1993 *Grey Area (Brown Version)*: five identical plaster Nefertiti busts in various shades are designed to raise questions about the racial identity of the ancient Egyptians.

14. Isa Genzken's 2012 *Nofretete:* seven sunglasses-wearing Nefertitis are used to raise questions about the place of women in art.

15. The Samalut roundabout Nefertiti. Intended as a tribute to Egypt's most beautiful queen, this version of Nefertiti was vilified on the internet, and was quickly removed.

The Man Who Gave Nefertiti Away: James Simon, the Forgotten Philanthropist, produced by journalist Carola Wedel,[25] a bronze portrait plaque now marks the site of Tiergartenstrasse 15a (the villa itself having been burned in 1933) and, as I write, the James Simon Gallery, designed by architect David Chipperfield, is rising on Museum Island, where it will serve as a much-needed visitor centre for the museums complex.

Displaying the Queen

In 1914 Pierre Lacau was appointed successor to Gaston Maspero as head of the Antiquities Service. He could not take up his position, however, until he had completed his war service. By 1919 the now strongly anti-German Lacau was in post and had started discussions with the British Egypt Exploration Fund (now the Egypt Exploration Society), who wished to take over the Amarna concession. Although unaware of the Nefertiti bust, Lacau was unhappy that the contents of the sculptor's workshop had been split, when they should really have been considered as one group: 'In that respect we have nothing specific to blame the Germans for; they have used the right the government had generously granted them at its own expense.'[26] He felt that the Antiquities Service should excavate the site, yet they were woefully overworked; he was therefore prepared to allow the EEF to excavate. There would, however, be no automatic 50:50 split of the finds. The EEF would receive only what the Service decided to allow them. The EEF were not happy, but when in 1920 Lacau informed them that a Harvard University mission was prepared to accept the new terms, they quickly agreed. In Britain at least, this was regarded as another albeit minor victory over the Germans. Borchardt, writing to James Quibell at the Cairo Museum, expressed his frustration with this outcome: 'The Egypt Exploration

Fund has been given our excavation site of Tell el-Amarna, and therefore shattered our hopes of conducting further work there.'[27]

In November 1922 Howard Carter discovered the long-lost tomb of Tutankhamen.[28] Tutankhamen had been something of an enigma: his name was known, but it was generally assumed that he was a long-serving member of the elite who claimed the throne after Akhenaten's death by marrying Nefertiti's third daughter, Ankhesen-paaten. This made him the son-in-law of Akhenaten and Nefertiti. His was the only near-intact tomb to be discovered in the Valley of the Kings, and it appeared to be filled with golden grave goods. The discovery came at a time when the Western world was still reeling from the Great War and the subsequent Spanish influenza pandemic. A desire for fun and distraction coexisted alongside an increased interest in religion and the occult, as the living struggled to maintain contact with their dead. Meanwhile new technologies allowed the transition of news quickly, allowing the general public to receive regular updates on events in the Valley of the Kings. As 'Tut-mania' erupted the Amarna Period – a period whose art and fashions sat so neatly alongside the contemporary art deco style, and whose quasi-monotheistic king appealed to those interested in ancient religions – became familiar as it had never been before.

With Amarna a lost cause, Schäfer lost patience with Borchardt's wish to keep the Nefertiti bust hidden. Photographs of the 'colourful queen' started to circulate, and in April 1924 she was added to the display in the newly opened Amarna Period hall. Here, her bust was rather unfortunately displayed in a small glass case with a black background that made it impossible to see the back of the sculpture. To facilitate this display, two metallic pins were inserted into the core of the bust through the base. The public was interested, but not overwhelmed.[29] At the same time, with no further reason to conceal his find, Borchardt published a book dedicated to images of Nefertiti, which included a full-plate coloured image of the bust in profile (right side, with the missing eye and more damaged ear hidden from view) and four other black-and-white plates showing the bust from various angles.[30] His publication also included an illustration and discussion of Lefebvre's painted stela, which he compared to a similar stela in the Neues Museum.

The Nefertiti bust quickly became a huge success. Would it have experienced the same success had it remained in Egypt and entered the collections of the Cairo Museum a decade earlier? Perhaps not. Lefebvre was not the only Egyptologist to resist the appeal of Akhenaten's art. As we have seen, many at the turn of the twentieth century considered Amarna sculpture to be atypical and even un-Egyptian, so that there is no guarantee that the contents of Thutmose's workshop would have been regarded as anything out of the ordinary. In 1913 the Cairo Museum did not have the overwhelming number of artefacts on display that it has today, but it was still packed with wondrous antiquities. And, as William Hutton observed as early as 1785, when reflecting on a visit to the British Museum, too many artefacts can be a bad thing for the visitor: 'If a man pass two minutes in a room, in which are a thousand things to demand his attention, he cannot find time to bestow on them a glance each.'[31]

Hutton's comments still ring true. Although there can be a calm beauty in a repetitive display, any museum which crams its galleries indiscriminately is in danger of overwhelming the casual visitor who becomes unable to see anything clearly.

Nefertiti's bust did not stand alone in Berlin; it had a supporting cast of choice Amarna artefacts. But the bust was very much the star of the museum, and the expectation was that all visitors would want to pay homage to Nefertiti. The 'museum effect' – the phenomenon that separating an object from its natural environment to display it in a museum gives that object a new importance and relevance – started to kick in.[32] And so, as the public arrived in ever increasing numbers to view the queen whom they were programmed to find beautiful, their very numbers sparked further interest in the bust. Ironically, the fact that the bust had been taken out of Egypt turned Nefertiti into an Egyptian national icon.

6

THE GERMAN QUEEN

She is, and remains, the ambassador of Egypt in Berlin.[1]

Hermann Parzinger, President of the SPK, speaking in 2011

News of the beautiful Nefertiti spread quickly beyond Germany's borders. On 17 February 1923 *The Illustrated London News* displayed what it claimed to be the first image of the bust; other British publications released the same image on the same day, also claiming to be the first with the news. Nefertiti was compared favourably with portraits of Cleopatra (presumably her coins, as few authentic Cleopatras have survived) and with the enigmatic smile of the Mona Lisa. Suddenly aware that '*les Boches*' had managed to acquire a great Egyptian treasure, Lacau took immediate action. He acknowledged that Borchardt had met all legal requirements, that the division had been properly documented with 'complete and accurate lists' and 'good photographs' and that the Antiquities Service was 'defenceless, legally speaking', yet he asked for the return of the bust on the grounds that there had obviously been a mistake in the division.

Whatever Lefebvre might have thought, the carved stela in the Cairo Museum did not have the artistic or historical merit of the Nefertiti bust: 'Isn't it clear that the bust is by far the more important piece and that the division being vitiated by an obvious error ought to be revised?'[2] Lacau approached Borchardt with a request for the return of the bust, only to be told that ownership had passed from Simon to the Neues Museum, and that the museum would not cooperate. As Borchardt blocked all further negotiation, in 1925 Lacau retaliated by stopping Borchardt from excavating until Germany either returned the bust or agreed to arbitration.

The matter was already being reported in the United Kingdom with varying degrees of accuracy in national and regional newspapers. On 22 March 1927 the *Scotsman* reported from Cairo that the Egyptian government had instructed their diplomatic representative in Berlin to reclaim the head, on the grounds that 'when Professor Borchardt, the German Egyptologist, removed it from the place of its discovery at Tel el-Amarna before the war, he did not declare its value to the Egyptian Customs authorities'. The British Foreign Office, concerned that the bust might become a test case, with Egypt demanding the repatriation of other artefacts, consulted Sir Frederick Kenyon of the British Museum, who took a firm line:

> *It is true that such an allocation is only explicable on the grounds of gross favouritism, incompetence or corruption on the part of their staff; but that is their affair, and they must take the consequences. The only justification, to my mind, of a claim for restitution would be if any deceit or concealment were practised by the Germans ... The mere argument that Egypt should have this object back because it has changed its mind is, I think, untenable, and should not be supported.*[3]

In January 1928 the Reichstag rejected the idea that the question of the bust should go to arbitration. Nevertheless, on 4 February 1928 the *Sphere* referred to the Berlin Museum as 'the present – but possibly temporary – resting-place of the great bust of … Nefertiti'. And on 13 April 1929 the same newspaper, under the headline 'To Arrange for the Arrival of a King and the Departure of a Queen', reported that the Egyptian Foreign Minister H. E. Hafiz Bey had arrived in Berlin to plan the visit of King Fuad, which was scheduled for May that year, and to negotiate for the return of the Nefertiti bust. King Fuad did make his planned visit, but the subject of the bust was not raised.[4]

Borchardt retired as director of the DOG in March 1929 and was replaced by Hermann Junker. There was a feeling on both sides that a deal might now be possible and so, in October 1929, Lacau travelled to Berlin to negotiate with Schäfer, who was now director of the Egyptian collection there. Initially Lacau suggested a straightforward swap: the bust for Lefebvre's painted stela plus sundry objects of lesser value. But Schäfer was not happy with this suggestion. Berlin already owned a carved stela depicting the royal family sitting beneath the rays of the Aten, and he felt that there was no need for another.[5] It was then proposed that in return for the Nefertiti bust, Berlin should receive two statues of acknowledged artistic and historical merit: a life-sized standing statue of the Old Kingdom high priest Ranefer and a sitting statue of the New Kingdom architect and priest Amenhotep, son of Hapu. The German Egyptologists were all agreed that this was an entirely reasonable exchange. Even without the bust, Berlin would have an exceptional Amarna display, and it would always be possible to add one of the replica busts, virtually indistinguishable from the original, that were now being created in ever increasing numbers in the Gipsformerei.

On 10 April 1930 the *Scotsman* was confidently reporting that 'as soon as the consent of the Egyptian and German authorities to the proposed exchange is obtained, Nefertiti will return to the land of her birth, and Berliners will no longer be able to admire her smile in Unter den Linden'. But German public opinion, roused by the press, was very much against the deal. The people of the Weimar Republic, having recently lost their own royal family, had been happy to claim Nefertiti as their own, so that the bust now functioned as what linguist Claudia Breger has described as 'an insignia of national identity'. She was a German queen and a German archaeological triumph, and they did not want to let her go.[6] Visitor numbers rocketed, and on 8 April *Der Tag* was able to report that the bust had 'received the honour of roses being laid down' before it.[7] At the last minute, the deal was called off.

Simon, as the former owner of the bust and founder of the DOG, was happy to make his own position clear. On 28 June 1930 he published an open letter in the evening edition of the *Berliner Tageblatt*, addressed to the Prussian Minister of Culture, Dr Grimme, reminding him that the museum's directors had promised that the bust would be returned to Egypt should the authorities ever request it. As a businessman, he felt that this promise should now be honoured. An exchange for items of equal worth would be a sensible solution that would save face, and would allow the DOG to continue its valuable excavation work:

> *There are quite a few objects in our collection, which from an artistic perspective, are more important than the elegantly colourful bust of the queen. However, there are other factors that contribute to its popularity with the public. This is an image of a really beautiful woman. And it is well known ... how easily the layman can confuse the beauty of the object with the value of its artistic representation. In my opinion, as far as art is concerned, one should guard against paying too much attention to public taste. Many of those who are now ranting the loudest about losing the bust have never seen it ... and are only now becoming so enthusiastic about*

it because fashion or even sensation has led them to the Egyptian Museum ...[8]

His letter was ignored. Angry and upset, Simon turned down his invitation to attend the opening of Berlin's Pergamon Museum; a museum whose contents, including the remarkable blue-tiled Ishtar Gate from Babylon, bore testament to his own generosity in financing archaeological missions. This was to be his last public intervention in the matter. Borchardt's views on the matter are unrecorded, but it may be that they are expressed in the 19,000-plus letters written between Borchardt and his wife, Emilie 'Mimi' Cohen Borchardt, which are currently stored, unread, in the Borchardts' Cairo villa, now home to the Swiss Archaeological Institute.[9] Borchardt had resumed his directorship of the DOG in 1923, but his excavating days were over. He died in Paris in 1938 and was buried in Cairo.

When, in October 1933, Hermann Göring, Minister of the Interior for Prussia, decided to give the Nefertiti bust to King Fuad, to commemorate the anniversary of his accession to the throne, the monarch was delighted. The German ambassador to Egypt, Eberhard von Stohrer, reports that he 'thanked me for this good news, and asked me to convey to the President, the Reich, Hindenburg, and the German government, his sincere thanks'. Adolf Hitler, however, was far from delighted, and personally intervened to block Nefertiti's return. More than a decade after the event, von Stohrer recalled Hitler's thoughts on Nefertiti:

Oh, these Egyptologists and these professors! I don't attach any value to their appraisals. I know this famous bust. I have viewed it and admired it many times ... It is a unique masterpiece, a jewel, a real treasure ... Do you know what I am going to do one day? I am going to build a new Egyptian Museum in Berlin; I dream that there I will create a hall topped by a dome, where alone, in the middle, this marvel will be placed. And for that reason, I will not renounce the queen's head.[10]

Hitler had an interest in Akhenaten's religion, which he saw as a form of pagan monotheism, associating the king with ideas of progress and a refusal to be bound by the past. There was something appealing about the ideal of a healthy life lived beneath the sun's rays and, while Akhenaten's appearance was not entirely comfortable for someone who appreciated the physically perfect, Nefertiti's bust fitted well with models of European health and beauty. Women could relate to Nefertiti and men could admire her. Nevertheless, Nefertiti made an unlikely role model for Nazi Germany.[11]

New York's *Jewish Daily Bulletin* picked up on this anomaly. Its edition published on 26 April 1934 makes grim reading. Page 1 has a brief article on the Nazi 'Race Fleet'; two hundred doctors who were to tour Germany explaining 'racial science' were given a send-off hosted by the Society for Racial Hygiene, an organisation dedicated to achieving racial 'purity' through selective reproduction and sterilisation. Page 3 reports 'the Ku Klux Klan riding again: Jews and Catholics are objects of their malignant activities'. On page 6 in the *Bulletin's* Day Book, we find an article on Nefertiti, or rather the Berlin bust version of Nefertiti:

> *Was Queen Nefertiti, dusky Egyptian beauty who shared the throne of the land of the pyramids, 'Aryan'? The question has stirred a lively dispute in one of the London newspapers after the Queen broke into print for having snared Adolf Hitler's heart … Not so long ago the Egyptian government, which is now intent on preserving for Egypt the relics of that land's past, requested the return of the bust for inclusion in the magnificent collection at Cairo. Herr Hitler, it is reported, does not wish Queen Nefertiti to leave Berlin because, in his own words, he is in love with her.*

In London's *Daily Telegraph*, the letters column was divided over whether Nefertiti had the power to conquer Hitler's heart, '*vincit omnia amor*', or whether, as some robustly maintained, Nefertiti was actually an Aryan princess. Many considered her name to be a vital clue to her origins. 'Nefertiti' – literally 'A Beautiful Woman has Come' – was not a particularly unusual name in ancient Egypt. It is likely to be a reference to arrival of the goddess Hathor. As Nefertiti appears wearing a Hathoric crown in the Theban Benben Temple, we may speculate that she adopted an appropriate name at the time of her marriage, in the same way than modern monarchs sometimes choose new names at the time of their coronation. But in the 1930s there was an assumption that the name referred to the arrival of the queen herself; that she had quite literally arrived at court as a beautiful woman, to marry Akhenaten. 'Nefertiti' would then be a replacement for an unpronounceable foreign name. Although there is no evidence for the arrival of a foreign bride at the start of Akhenaten's reign, the harem that he inherited from his father did house several age-appropriate princesses. The most likely of these was Tadukhepa, daughter of Tushratta of Mitanni. Tadukhepa had been sent to Egypt to marry Amenhotep III but her arrival coincided with the death of her elderly bridegroom. We know that she remained in Egypt to marry Akhenaten, but from this point on she disappears from view. On the basis of this very flimsy evidence, many accepted that Nefertiti must be Tadukhepa.

Nefertiti was not the only Amarna queen to be identified as non-Egyptian. When, in 1912, John Player and Co. produced a set of twenty-five 'Egyptian Kings and Queens and Classical Deities' cigarette cards, the collection included King Amenophis (Amenhotep III) and his consort, 'Queen Amenophis' (Queen Tiy). The queen, seen in profile wearing the vulture headdress, a golden collar and a somewhat un-Egyptian looking green dress, is described as being 'of Asiatic origin ... she was blue eyed and of very fair complexion and tenderly loved by her husband'. Her cartouche was rendered correctly, and the names of her parents were given more or less correctly as 'Juas and Tuaa'. Nefertiti, a virtual unknown at this time, did not merit a cigarette card.[12] The idea that Tiy was a blue-eyed blonde from Mitanni had been developed by Petrie, who based his conclusions on her physiognomy and felt confident enough in his analysis to declare that 'The source then of this [Akhenaten's] peculiar face is the Mitannian blood of his mother Thyi.'[13] The discovery of the entirely Egyptian tomb of Tiy's parents, Yuya and Thuyu, in the Valley of the Kings in 1905 should have put an end to this idea.[14] But no one told John Player and Co., and so the misinformation continued to spread.

If Tiy had been an Aryan princess married to an Egyptian king, Akhenaten himself would have been half-Aryan. As the aforementioned *Jewish Daily Bulletin* pointed out, that would not have been enough to satisfy Hitler:

This is an impossible state of affairs. If Herr Hitler is going to admit publicly his love for a woman of doubtful 'Aryanism' who remained married to a 'half Aryan' (which, to all Nazi intents, is 'non-Aryan') he condones the same failing in his 'Aryan' subjects. What's good for the Führer is good for the follower. We logically expect, therefore, an end to this agitation against marriage between 'Aryans' and 'non-Aryans' and the issuance of instructions from the Brown House to the German cupid that he may once again shoot his arrows where he will without first referring to Dr Achim Gercke and his racial records of approval of his targets.

But this seemed all wrong:

Well, this department looked at a photograph of Queen Nefertiti but perhaps because we haven't had the training that Herr Hitler's race detection department has had, it didn't clarify matters. The Queen (from the photograph) is a robust, Semitic-looking woman who, if dressed in modern clothes and with a modified head-dress, might be a resident of West End Avenue and a member of the Women's Division of the American Jewish Congress.

The Second World War

The Amarna artefacts remained on display until, in August 1939, with war imminent, the Berlin Museums were forced to close. The precious collections were packed up and transferred to secure locations in monasteries, castles, mines and tunnels. This was to prove a wise precaution. All the buildings on Museum Island were to suffer war damage, with more than a third of the Neues Museum being destroyed during a Royal Air Force raid in 1943. The bust, stored in a crate labelled THE COLOURFUL QUEEN, was moved first to the vault of the Prussian Governmental Bank and then, in 1941, to a flak bunker near Berlin zoo. Finally, shortly before the Red Army took Berlin in 1945, the bust was hidden 'by order of the Führer' alongside Germany's gold and currency reserves in a salt mine at Merkers-Kieselbach in Thuringia.[15] When, five months later, the mine was captured by the Allied forces, the bust passed to the Monuments, Fine Arts, and Archives branch of the US Army. It was sent first to the Reichsbank in Frankfurt, and then to the US Central Collection Point in Wiesbaden, which was headed by the trained architect Captain Walter I. Farmer. Farmer prided himself on treating the objects in his care with appropriate reverence and respect, protecting them from the curious and guarding them from damage. He was therefore horrified to learn that, in December 1945, while he was on leave in England, the crate containing the head had been opened specifically against his instructions:

Even today I have no clear explanation of what happened. One story is that Joe Kelleher [Captain Patrick J. Kelleher] had arranged a dinner party and afterwards for entertainment had offered his guests a thrilling experience. They were given a private showing of the famous portrait bust of the Egyptian Queen Nefertiti. Despite my orders as director of the Collecting Point that none of the Berlin Museum crates should ever be opened without my authorisation, Joe Kelleher had ordered the well sealed box to be opened. Frau Hobirk, of the German staff, was called in to lift her out; if she fell an American would not be at fault ... When I confronted Kelleher with my knowledge that the box had been opened he swore that he had been ordered by two generals to open it for their inspection.[16]

Subsequently this story mutated into the rumour that the Americans had unpacked the bust to raise a glass to Nefertiti on Christmas Day. Farmer strongly objected to this story: 'Nefertiti was indeed a queen, and while she was our guest should have been shown every regal courtesy.' Liberated from her protective crate, Nefertiti became something of a liability, as increasing numbers of visitors started to drop by and ask for a glimpse of the famous queen. This may have prompted Farmer's decision to hold an exhibition of German-owned artefacts, designed to reassure the German people that the Americans were looking after their treasures properly. In 1946 the Nefertiti bust went on public display in Wiesbaden.

That same year saw a request for the repatriation of the bust, addressed by the Egyptian government to the Allied Control Commission in Germany, reminding them that the previous return of the bust had been thwarted only by Hitler, who had declared that the bust would never be returned because '*il en était amoureux*'.[17] With Hitler defeated, there was no reason not to right an historic wrong. A copy of this request was sent by the Egyptian ambassador to the British Foreign Office, who responded that they could do nothing to intervene in the matter. The Metropolitan Museum felt that perhaps the bust could be sent via New York to Egypt, where it could be displayed as restitution for damage caused during the war. It is due largely to Farmer's intervention that the Americans rejected this plan and refused the repatriation of the bust, on the grounds that they could only repatriate objects looted during the war. This was a legal matter between the Egyptians and the Germans, and 'it is assumed that, subsequent to the re-establishment of a competent German government, this case may be brought to the attention of such government'.[18]

The Wiesbaden Collection Point was responsible for the collecting, cataloguing and returning the artworks stored by the Nazis. By December 1950 some 340,846 items – an item in some cases being an entire library – had been returned to the countries from which they had been taken, while many thousands still awaited processing.[19] The artefacts from the Berlin Museums presented a particular problem as, following the collapse of the Reich, Berlin had become a divided city. In 1956 the Nefertiti bust was sent not to the Neues Museum but to West Berlin. It was exhibited first in the Dahlem Museum before moving, in 1967, to the Egyptian Museum in Berlin-Charlottenburg. Here, almost overnight, the bust, isolated from its original environment and dislocated from much of the Berlin Egyptology collection, became a symbol for isolated West Berlin. Meanwhile the German Democratic Republic tried to claim the bust on the grounds that its former home, the Neues Museum on Museum Island, was located in East Berlin. This bitter dispute only ended in 1990, when the Berlin wall fell and the two Germanys became one.

Following reunification, the Nefertiti bust was temporarily displayed in the Altes Museum as 'Master Plan Museum Island' – the complete restoration of the Island as a modern complex suitable for the needs of modern visitors – got underway. The Neues Museum, originally designed by Friedrich Auguste Stüler and now re-envisaged by David Chipperfield, reopened in 2009. Today the Nefertiti bust is once again its star exhibit. Outside the museum, Nefertiti now symbolises the united Berlin, and her bust has featured on stamps, postcards and billboards, often with her missing eye restored. There have been repeated requests for her return to Egypt – in 1984, for example, the Nefertiti Wants to Go Home movement, led by Herbert Ganslmayr and Gert von Paczensky, suggested that the bust be displayed alternately in Cairo and Berlin, while in 2005 Egypt appealed to UNESCO to resolve the dispute – but the German authorities have stood firm.

The Beautiful Woman Returns?

The question of whether Western institutions should return foreign works of art and antiquity seized, purchased or otherwise obtained under what today may be classified as imperialist conditions is one that haunts many museums. It is a question fraught with complexity.[20] The originating countries usually want some, if not all, of their 'plundered' treasures to be returned, while the museums wish to retain 'their' collections intact, see the treasures as belonging to the world rather than to one country, and fear that even one return might set a dangerous precedent.

In the case of obviously stolen works, almost everyone is in agreement. Reputable museums will not willingly acquire or display non-provenanced artefacts, and if an artefact is identified as stolen it will be returned without argument to its legal owner.[21] Nefertiti's bust was not, however, obviously stolen. It was acquired in accordance with then current Egyptian law as part of a legitimate division of finds, and its legal owner has been, since 1957, the SPK. Many would agree that its acquisition was opportunistic to say the least, and that the Antiquities Service represented by Lefebvre was negligent, but it is difficult to argue that it was illegal unless it is also argued that Borchardt, with deliberate intent, was able to exert such undue influence over Lefebvre as to make the division void.

Lefebvre's decision to reject the Nefertiti bust had no obvious effect on his career. Following the Great War he became assistant curator at the Cairo Museum before replacing Pierre Lacau on his retirement in 1926. When Lacau asked questions about the division, Lefebvre prudently stated that he could not remember whether or not he had seen the bust.[22] We therefore have to guess what went through his mind during what to us seems to have been a momentous event, but what was for him simply another day at the office. Although we know that Lefebvre was charged with selecting the finds that the Antiquities Service wished to retain, we do not know the grounds on which he was expected to made his selection. As a linguist, he may have been on the look-out for inscribed pieces that would untangle some of the complexities of the Amarna Period. The Nefertiti bust was an ideal, crowd-pleasing museum piece, but it lacked the inscriptions that would have advanced understanding. The unusual decoration may have seemed gaudy and brash to eyes more accustomed to unpainted stone, while its missing eye marked the bust as broken or incomplete. As the Cairo Museum already had a sizeable collection of royal heads, Lefebvre may have felt that to add the unlabelled bust of an unremarkable queen to the collection was unnecessary. The painted and inscribed stone stela, on the other hand, was an object of beauty in its own right, and one that did promise a deeper understanding of the Amarna Period.

To many, Lefebvre's failure to select Nefertiti for Egypt is so inexplicable that it cannot have been the result of indifference or incompetence. There must have been trickery or outright criminality involved. Claims that Borchardt misappropriated the Nefertiti bust have been rife, and so well publicised that even in Germany

many people unthinkingly accept that it was stolen. The bust regularly appears on lists of looted artefacts in popular publications and so here, for example, included at number five on the *Guardian* newspaper's list of 'the 10 most notorious looted artworks', we find:

> *Limestone bust of Queen Nefertiti, c 1345, by the sculptor Thutmose. While he was digging at Amarna in 1912, the German archaeologist Ludwig Borchardt discovered this bust and stole it. Under the established procedure of 'partage' he was meant to declare all items to an official of the Antiquities Service in Tell el Amarna, so a fair split could be made. But he did not declare her.*[23]

The more sensational claims – that the bust was smuggled out of Egypt in a basket of fruit, or that it was disguised below a thick layer of clay that rendered it unrecognisable – can be rejected as they contradict the known facts. Lacau was happy to accept that the division had been conducted appropriately, and that his representative had made a simple error. Borchardt himself always maintained to his own family that the bust was properly obtained.[24] Güterbock, our helpful eyewitness, summarises the situation from the dig director's perspective:

> *Nefertiti's bust has not at all been hidden from the representative of the Egyptian Administration of Antiquities; it was shown to him in photograph 18/24, and subsequently he was shown the original. In the protocol of the division, it is listed at the top as No. 1.*[25]

So far so well but, as he concedes: 'No excavator is obliged to almost point out the beauty of his finds.'[26] It seems that Borchardt, while obeying the letter of the law, did not take it upon himself to make Lefebvre's job easy, and there is one area where his behaviour invites our scrutiny. The official division protocol, written in French, listed the head as '*Buste en plâtre peinte d'une princesse de la famille royale*' [Bust in painted plaster of a princess of the royal family]. It is not clear who created this description, but it contains two major errors. The fact that Nefertiti is listed as a princess rather than a queen is odd, but this distinction would have meant less in 1913 than it does today. The fact that the bust is listed as being made of plaster is more significant. The outer layer of the bust is, indeed, gypsum or plaster; its core, however, is limestone. It is possible that the piece was deliberately misdescribed because Lefebvre had agreed in advance of the division that all the plaster heads should go to Germany; as it turned out, Lefebvre was also content to allow the stone heads to leave Egypt. Why Lefebvre thought it acceptable to reject the plaster heads *en bloc* – some of the most poignant and potentially informative pieces of art ever to be recovered from the dynastic age – is rarely questioned.

The misdirection/mistake in the protocol, and the fact that Lefebvre was shown the Amarna artefacts under far from ideal conditions, suggest that Borchardt was guilty of hoping to retain the bust for his German patron. However, this does not shift the responsibility for the decision from Lefebvre. As the representative of the Antiquities Service, it was his duty to examine all finds properly, in a good light, and then make his selection. If he did rely on the excavator's notes and photographs, if he failed to make a thorough examination of each and every artefact, and if he failed to realise that a dig director might not necessarily display everything in the best possible light, he failed in his duty. This would be unfortunate, but it would not make the division illegal. Nevertheless, this evidence has been used to argue for the return of the bust. In January 2011 Dr Zahi Hawass, then head of Egypt's Supreme Council of Antiquities (the former Antiquities Service) under the Mubarak government, issued a formal request for Nefertiti's return. Citing Article 33(b) of the UNESCO Convention on the Means of Prohibiting and

Preventing the Illicit Import, Export and Transfer of Ownership of Cultural Property (1970), he argued that 'this request is a natural consequence of Egypt's long-standing policy of seeking the restitution of all archaeological artefacts that have been taken illicitly out of the country'. As the request had not been signed by the Egyptian prime minister, the German authorities did not consider it to be an official repatriation request, and turned it down. The Arab Spring brought this discussion to an abrupt end, but it has continued sporadically under successive regimes.

If Germany has a strong legal case to support its ownership of the bust, the moral case is far less clear. Is it ever right that one country should own another country's cultural assets? To the Egyptians, Nefertiti's bust has become a symbol of a lost – or stolen – heritage, seized at a time when Egypt was helpless under foreign rule. That the bust has the power to provoke powerful reactions in Egypt can be seen by the immediate, media-fuelled, response to the massive, ill-crafted replica that was, in 2015, erected on a roundabout at the entrance to the city of Samalut. Twitter was quick to dub the image 'an insult to Nefertiti and to every Egyptian', and comparisons were drawn with Frankenstein's monster. The statue had to be withdrawn after a few days, to be replaced by a dove of peace.

To the Germans, Nefertiti's post-Amarna adventures are a valid part of her history that cannot be erased by returning her to Egypt. It is her sojourn in Germany that has made Nefertiti the celebrity that she is today, and Egypt actively benefits from her presence in Berlin, where she acts as an ambassador, promoting Egypt and creating understanding and respect for cultural diversity. Hermann Parzinger, president of the SPK, has summarised this view: 'Nefertiti is part of humanity's cultural heritage. I fundamentally do not think that restituting the bust simply for generosity's sake is justifiable.'[27] Economically, the Berlin Museum certainly benefits from the tourists who queue to see the bust. Does Egypt then benefit from those same tourists, who decide to visit Nefertiti's homeland? In the Cairo Museum, alongside the golden treasures of Tutankhamen and the silver treasures of Tanis, Nefertiti's aura would surely diminish. But in Egypt she would be accessible to at least some of the Egyptian people who currently cannot see her.

In 2003 Little Warsaw's installation *The Body of Nefertiti* led to a new demand for the bust's return. This was less a legal or moral argument than a cultural one. To the Egyptian authorities, the Germans were endangering the safety of a priceless artefact and, more importantly, treating their queen with the utmost disrespect by allowing her to participate in a trivial artistic experiment. To the German authorities, the Egyptians were expressing the view that Nefertiti should be placed in a sterile cultural vacuum which would exclude her from the modern world. Stephen K. Urice, an expert in cultural property law, has summed up this argument:

> *What Egypt's reaction to The Body of Nefertiti makes clear, is that a return of the bust to Egypt would place it out of the reach of contemporary artists such as Little Warsaw. The bust holds absolutely no place in current Egyptian religious practice and no appreciable use in developing or maintaining current Egyptian national identity. Were it to be returned to Egypt, it would likely be isolated from the stream of creative expression to which it can contribute and from which it can derive new meaning. To condemn the bust to such an existence is ... to assure that the bust remain forevermore beautiful but dead.*[28]

Urice is here responding to a request that he and fellow legal expert Kurt G. Siehr should take opposing positions on the question of whether the Nefertiti bust should remain in Berlin or be returned to Egypt. As Siehr makes clear 'As lawyers, both of us might have argued either position.'[29]

As early as 1927 Arthur Weigall had raised the subject of the bust's safety should it be returned to Egypt:

> *The German scholars of the Berlin Museum are probably better trained than are their French, English and Egyptian confrères who manage the Cairo Museum; and Berlin is a city perhaps less liable to a destructive upheaval than is the Egyptian capital.*[30]

Weigall, lacking the gift of foresight, was entirely wrong in regarding the Neues Museum as a more secure environment than its Cairene counterpart. But he was asking a question that others have since raised. Does it makes sense to put all of ancient Egypt's archaeological eggs into one basket that a fire, an earthquake or sudden civil unrest could entirely destroy? The 2011 Arab Spring saw the plundering of the Cairo Museum gift shop, which was apparently mistaken for the actual museum, and the loss and subsequent recovery of some of Tutankhamen's grave goods from the museum itself. This has encouraged many to see the West as the protector of some of Egypt's heritage. Hawass's suggestion that Nefertiti might be displayed in the new Akhenaten Museum in Minya, close to her original Amarna home, might avoid this problem. But Middle Egypt is desperately short of tourists and, since the neighbouring Malawi Museum was ransacked and torched during the Arab Spring, many consider it to be dangerously insecure.

As I write, Egypt is asking that the Nefertiti bust be returned to Egypt on loan for the opening of Grand Egyptian Museum at Giza, which is scheduled for 2018. This is a repeat request; in 2007, Hawass asked that the bust be returned for three months to feature at the opening of the museum, which was then scheduled for 2011. The German authorities have always declared the bust too fragile to travel. Hawass has responded by suggesting that the bust be examined by an independent panel of experts:

Given the immeasurable delight and pride which this object could bring to the Egyptians who have never had the opportunity to see it, it seems that a thorough and impartial evaluation by a scientific committee is called for to be sure that every possible scenario for its safe display in Egypt has been exhausted before our request for [its] loan is denied. We would never endanger any of our treasures by insisting that they travel against the advice of an impartial commission of experts. However, we do maintain that the evaluation of these objects should be carried out by a balanced and diverse international committee, including experts from Egypt and from other non-Western nations.[31]

It seems unlikely, given Egypt's often-declared view that the Nefertiti bust is stolen property, that the Germans will ever consider it fit to travel. As Hawass has stated: 'They fear it will be like *Raiders of the Lost Ark*, and we will take it and not give it back.'[32]

7

MULTIPLE NEFERTITIS

Archaeology and art masterpieces do not mix.[1]

Professor Barry Kemp (2012)

In the early 1920s, before the Nefertiti bust was put on public display, Heinrich Schäfer, Director of the Egyptian Museum and Papyrus Collection in Berlin, commissioned Tina Haim-Wentscher to make a third, very accurate replica to accompany the two she had already produced for James Simon some ten years earlier. This she did working alongside the original, using callipers to take multiple measurements.[2] For many years Haim's interpretation of the Nefertiti bust served as the 'model' for all the replicas issued by the Gipsformerei, or replica workshop, of the Berlin Museum. Many of the myriad high-quality Nefertitis that can be found in museums worldwide are plaster casts of Haim's sculpture; their paintwork replicates Haim's own rather than the original's.[3] Other replicas, ever so slightly different in appearance, particularly in regard to their treatment of the eyes, are based on later models created either freehand or, more recently, from laser scans.[4] In 2015 the most recent official model of the Nefertiti bust was created using modern scanning technologies that allowed accuracy to a tenth of a millimetre. Following a comparative analysis of the paint on the original bust, this model was painted using original pigments and traditional painting techniques. A rock crystal was used to create the right eye.

The Berlin Gipsformerei is a remarkable survival from a bygone age. Founded in 1819 by Friedrich Wilhelm III, it became a part of Berlin's Royal Museums (now the Staatliche Museen zu Berlin) in 1830. It was not unique: throughout the nineteenth century plaster-cast workshops were seen as a vital element in the museum structure, and all the major Western museums employed artists to create high-quality plaster replicas of the key pieces in their collections. These casts allowed museums to disseminate accurate information about their own collections while generating a useful income stream. The casts were sent to national and provincial museums, where they were either displayed in dedicated cast courts or placed on the galleries alongside genuinely ancient artefacts so that the unwary visitor must have struggled to differentiate between the real and the replica artefacts. Plaster casts were employed in school and university teaching, and were acquired as works of art in their own right by private individuals, some of whom amassed impressively large collections. While museums were unwilling to lend their ancient artefacts, fearing, perhaps, that their treasures would not be returned, they were happy to sell and exchange casts. When in 1798 Napoleon's troops looted the Papal States and seized their artworks, the French offered plaster casts in compensation. The British Museum made casts of the Parthenon frieze available in 1819.[5]

The twentieth century saw a reaction against the displaying of 'fakes' in museums, which led to the closure of many of the cast courts and the dispersal or destruction of their collections. However, opinion has once again shifted, and today the original Victorian casts are appreciated both as works of art in their own right and as impressive technical achievements.[6] While other museums have closed their replica workshops, the Gipsformerei continues to thrive with a staff of twenty-four highly skilled artists dedicated to creating hand-crafted, museum-grade replicas. The Gipsformerei is, however, far more than a commercial workshop. It has become an important historic archive holding almost 7,000 models and casts plus a collection of antique plaster moulds, some of which represent our only link to lost, badly damaged or over-restored artefacts.[7]

The traditional replica manufacturing process started with the creation of a plaster mould from either the original sculpture or, in the case of fragile or painted pieces such as the Nefertiti bust, an accurate model. As sculptures almost invariably include indentations and projections, this mould had to be created in several pieces. Next, the piece-mould was enclosed in an outer casing, the interior of the mould was washed with a separating agent to prevent sticking, and a high-quality plaster was poured in. Once the plaster had set, the cast was released from its mould and lightly sanded to remove the casting lines between the mould pieces. While some casts were simply polished, the Nefertiti bust had to be hand painted, with the artist not only copying the colours but also replicating all areas of damage. As they are all hand painted, no two Nefertiti replica busts can ever be exactly alike, and none can ever be exactly the same as the original. The Gipsformerei still uses the traditional piece-moulds to create replicas from high-quality plaster of Paris but this is a slow and expensive way of working, and new technologies have been added to the repertoire. Silicone moulds now allow the more rapid replication of more popular pieces, while structured-light 3D scans allow the manufacture of non-contact models using a 3D printer.

The Gipsformerei recreated several of the Amarna heads in plaster, but it was the Nefertiti bust which attracted most attention and which earned the most money. Initially, the bust was only supplied in the white, unpainted version. When a painted version did become available, it was possible to make requests such as the adding of the left eye. As the various replica Nefertitis spread out from Berlin, visitors were attracted in the opposite direction, intent on seeing the original of a piece that was already very familiar to them. By November 1924 a colourful, one-eyed replica was drawing crowds to the British Museum, where it was displayed alongside genuine artefacts in a wall-case in the Egyptian gallery. On 9 December 1925 *The Times* carried a brief paragraph: a subtle advert designed to draw visitors to Harrods store in London:

> 1,400 BC
> It's hard to realise there was a world at all then, but I did the other day when I saw at Harrods the reproduction of a painted limestone head of Queen Nefertiti. You should see this bust, for I hear it is one of the only two reproductions in the world today and has been specially lent to Harrods by a well-known Egyptologist.
> Harrods Ground Floor
> Lady Babs

'Lady Babs' was, of course, wrong; there were already many versions of the Nefertiti bust in circulation. She had even reached Lancashire. On 1 December of that same year George Carpenter, keeper of Egyptology and archaeology at the Manchester Museum, wrote to Thomas Midgley, curator of the Chadwick Museum in nearby Bolton, on precisely this subject. Midgley had been inquiring about a replica Nefertiti bust, which he had admired in the Manchester collection. Carpenter was able to advise him that the bust had been purchased from the Berlin Museum for £4 including reparations duty plus £2 5s 6d transport and insurance. The bust arrived in

Bolton in February 1926, and its unveiling in the Chadwick Museum was reported in the local newspaper.[8] After some confusion over reclaiming the war reparations, Midgely calculated that the replica had cost £3 8s 6d plus a reparation levy of 26 per cent and shipping charges. This was a good investment. As I write this in 2017 a hand-painted, life-sized Nefertiti bust created from the 2015 model can be bought from the Gipsformerei for €8,900 with a choice of plinth (light Persian shell limestone, or black granite); an unpainted version costs €1,290. When the Chadwick Museum closed in 1956 the Nefertiti bust was transferred to the new Bolton Museum and Art Gallery, where it was displayed alongside the genuine but unspectacular Amarna artefacts that represented Bolton's share of the division acquired by the Egypt Exploration Society.

Fakes and Mistakes

As a child I believed that the Haim replica in the Bolton Museum was a genuine antiquity. As a one-time museum professional who has spent many hours patrolling the Egyptology galleries in the Manchester Museum, I know that many museum visitors make this same mistake. The label may make it clear that the bust is a replica, but surprisingly few visitors read museum labels carefully. The replica looks old and slightly battered, and its presence within the museum – seen by many as an academically sacred space dedicated to truth – is confusing: we tend to assume that the things we are shown in museums are 'real'. Aware of this, the Manchester Museum has recently gone from one extreme to another. Its Haim replica is now separated from the Egyptology collection, and is displayed in a case boldly and quite inappropriately labelled 'Fakes'. In contrast the Tyrannosaurus rex skeleton known as 'Stan' is still on display and is one of the museum's most popular attractions. Few who visit the dinosaur in his gallery, or read about him on the museum's website, are likely to realise that he is a plaster cast, and that the original Stan is housed in the Black Hills Institute of Geological Research in South Dakota.

To some observers, it is the original Nefertiti bust that is the fake, commissioned by Borchardt and, perhaps, modelled on his wife Mimi.[9] Swiss author and historian Henri Stierlin has developed an elaborate argument to support this theory, which has gained a surprising degree of acceptance amongst alternative Egyptologists and on the internet. In Stierlin's version of events, the bust was created by sculptor Gerhard Marcks to test the use of ancient pigments. After it had been admired by Prince Johann Georg of Saxony, Borchardt did not feel that he could reveal its true nature without making the prince look foolish. He therefore sent the bust to Berlin with the genuine Amarna artefacts, and then tried very hard to persuade the museum not to put it on display. There is an element of truth in this tale. Prince Johann Georg and his wife Maria Immaculata did pay an unexpected visit to Amarna on 6 December 1912, with the prince later recording details of the visit in his diary. But the prince makes no specific mention of the bust:

> *The men had intended to excavate just one house where they suspected there might be some finds ... Instead, a gentleman sent a note in the morning, before we arrived, that he believed he had found something interesting, and so it was. It turned out to be a sculptor's atelier, where we saw around 20 well-preserved busts that had been dug out, among them some very valuable showpieces.*[10]

Bolton sculptor Shaun Greenhalgh also feels that the bust is a fake, on the grounds that the selective distribution of the damage, which is observable on the ears, the back of the head and the uraeus but not on the nose, is incompatible with its being an ancient artefact. Describing Nefertiti as 'a beautiful Edwardian lady, done up in Egyptian make-up', he condemns the plaster exterior as the work of either an amateur or a second- or third-rate sculptor. The one surviving eye, however, he classifies as real; an ancient element added to a modern forgery to make it more acceptable to the experts. The fact that there is one eye rather than two is simply an indication that the forger could not source a pair.[11]

Greenhalgh, just one year younger than me, was another child inspired by the atmospheric Egyptian gallery in Bolton Museum. Our careers, however, took different turns. In 2006 Greenhalgh was revealed as the unlikely master-craftsman behind the 'Amarna Princess', a fraud that deceived the Egyptological world, and persuaded Bolton Museum to pay £439,767 for what was believed to be the broken yet still beautiful statue of one of Nefertiti's daughters.[12] The mechanics of the fraud were elegantly simple. Working in partnership with his parents, Greenhalgh obtained a copy of the 1892 unillustrated catalogue detailing the sale of the contents of Silverton Park in Devon. This included the tantalisingly vague description of a partial lot: 'eight Egyptian figures'. After three weeks working in his shed, Greenhalgh had produced an Amarna-style female torso, closely modelled on an Amarna sculpture in the Louvre. His statue was dressed in a clinging, pleated garment, and the remains of a 'sidelock' hairstyle suggested that she was a princess rather than a queen. Greenhalgh had made his princess from calcite, using modern DIY tools; layers of tea and clay had been applied to give it the appropriate patina of age. Greenhalgh's octogenarian father approached Bolton Museum armed with the statue (casually carried in a rucksack), the catalogue, and a (forged) letter supported his claim that the statue, bought from the sale by his mill-owning great-grandfather, had been in the family for over a century. Stunned by the totally unexpected arrival of a seemingly genuine alabaster Amarna princess in her office, Bolton Museum curator Angela

Thomas sought advice from the British Museum and, after close inspection, the statue was declared genuine. The princess – a fake by anyone's definition of the word – stood with her true nature unrecognised alongside the slightly older replica Nefertiti bust and the considerably older Amarna artefacts for three years.

In 2006 the Greenhalgh family attempted to sell a group of Assyrian reliefs to the British Museum. These, too, had apparently come from the Silverton Park sale as documented in the 1892 catalogue. However, a close examination by an expert employed by Bonhams Auction House showed that the reliefs contained numerous stylistic errors. The Metropolitan Police were informed, and requested that Bolton Museum re-examine their princess. This re-examination revealed anomalies which could be considered within the bounds of acceptability when the statue had a firm provenance, but which became of far greater significance when that provenance was removed. There were oddities in the sculpting; the knot tying the dress under the right breast was not well formed; the neckline hem had a unique finishing; the left arm was disproportionately slender; and there was carving on the negative space by the left leg, which should not have been there as the negative space was not considered to be a part of the sculpture. The stone, too, was not quite right: it was a strangely homogeneous colour with air bubbles apparent in the weathering; it was soft enough to be damaged by a thumbnail and therefore unlikely to have lasted 3,000 years relatively unscathed; and it showed a curious wear pattern. The chances were that the princess was a forgery. The experts who declared it genuine had been distracted by its faked provenance, and had neglected to look at the piece itself.

When the 'princess' was impounded by the police, there was a mood of disquiet in Bolton. While no one argued that the fraud was a good thing – £439,767 is a huge sum of money that could have been used to safeguard other heritage items – there was a general feeling that the Greenhalgh sculpture represented a poor local boy beating the experts at their own game. Furthermore, it raised interesting questions. If the princess was beautiful enough to be purchased, put on display and admired by many hundreds of visitors, did she not retain that beauty when the truth was revealed? Or, as the 'experts' believed, did her beauty stem solely from her authenticity? To many Bolton residents, the history of the Amarna princess was as interesting and relevant, if not more interesting and relevant, as the history of the genuine pieces displayed on the museum gallery, because the princess had a direct link to Bolton. When in 2011 the princess returned to Bolton as part of the Metropolitan Police's touring *Fakes and Forgeries* exhibition, she proved more popular than ever before.

Greenhalgh's expertise as a forger of ancient Egyptian sculpture is unrivalled (or so museum curators like to think). However, his identification of the Nefertiti bust as a fake does not sit well with the various contemporary and near-contemporary written accounts of its discovery and the subsequent division. Not does it fit with the fact that the bust was recovered as part of a collection of similarly themed sculptures, including a companion bust of Akhenaten. It is not easy to date a stone artefact as one runs the risk of simply dating the stone, but the pigments used to colour the bust have been analysed, and have been found to be entirely consistent with later Eighteenth Dynasty usage. Finally, the recent CT scans, which have revealed the bust's complex inner structure, tell us that the piece would have taken many hours to create. It is highly unlikely that a copyist, or even a dedicated forger, commissioned or otherwise, would go to so much trouble. We can therefore dismiss the suggestion that the bust is a forgery masterminded by Borchardt, and with it the equally elaborate conspiracy theory that sees the bust now on display as a replica created by Hitler. This theory, which is again perennially popular online, maintains that Hitler, wishing to form an alliance with the Egyptians, had a replica made to be presented to the country after Germany had triumphed in the Second World War. Unknown to the Egyptians, the real Nefertiti would have remained in Berlin. When the Neues Museum was emptied, the busts were stored in identical crates. Then, during the muddled aftermath of the war, the crate holding the genuine bust was lost, leaving the fake bust to be recovered by the Americans.

An additional complication is introduced to our story by the suggestion that, although the Nefertiti bust is a genuine antiquity, the small painted stela which topped Lefebvre's list of finds, and which is now displayed in the Cairo Museum, is a fake. This theory has been discussed by Rolf Krauss, who has suggested that Borchardt had the stela manufactured to distract Lefebvre's attention from the bust during the division.[13] It is true that the stela is strikingly similar to an Amarna stela of unknown provenance in the Berlin Museum collection.[14] Both stelae show the royal family – Akhenaten, Nefertiti and the three older princesses – sitting beneath the rays of the Aten. Both were presumably created as objects of private worship for the Amarna elite. It is therefore likely that, rather than one being a copy of the other, both were copied, somewhat loosely, from a model. Alongside a meticulous analysis of the scenes on both stelae, Krauss offers an anecdote recorded by the renowned linguist Adolf Erman, who taught Borchardt the cuneiform script in 1887–8:

> *[Borchardt] made a clay tablet which was completely akin to the authentic ones with the exception that it contained logarithms in cuneiform numbers. Borchardt put the tablet into a box with genuine tablets which were studied by the Assyriologist Peiser. The latter and a colleague were enthusiastic when they deciphered the tablet.*[15]

The hoax was only halted when Borchardt confessed, leaving Peiser, who had been about to publish the text, angry and embarrassed. So could the Amarna stela have been faked by Borchardt, on site? Time and access to raw materials would be crucial here. The bust was discovered on 6 December 1912; the painted stela was discovered on 11 January 1913, lying behind house Q47.16, buried just beneath 20cm (8in) of sand. Krauss suggests that this left enough time for Borchardt to order and receive a plaster cast of the Berlin stela, and to have it replicated and then planted on site. However, he points out that for the deception to succeed, the workman who uncovered the stela, his foreman Abdulhassan, the expedition member who supervised Abdulhassan, and possibly Ranke, who entered the stela into the official dig diary, would all have to have been involved. This seems an awful lot of people to hold a very big secret.

Just how long would it have taken to create either the fake or the original bust? In order to get some idea of the enormity of the task, and to allow me to gain a better understanding of the manufacturing process in Thutmose's workshop, my brother, Frank Tyldesley, valiantly offered to carve a replica Nefertiti for me. This was not to be an exact copy – that would have been impossible, as Frank could not work alongside the original bust – but it would be of equal size and a close likeness based on measurements taken from a model obtained via a 3D photocopy scanned from one of the official replicas cast from the Haim bust, and it would allow me to see Nefertiti again emerge from a block of stone. Frank is not a professional sculptor but an experienced amateur with an entirely different and time-consuming job; this meant that the hours available to work on his Nefertiti would be limited. And his access to authentic tools would be limited too. Although he worked by hand, Frank used modern, tungsten-tipped tools, primarily the chisel and the rasp. Thutmose's workmen would have used stone, wooden, copper and bronze tools, and would not have had access to iron. The comparatively soft local limestone of the Berlin bust would have been easier to work then Frank's Portland limestone, although it did contain some flint inclusions which may have made things more difficult.

Frank soon regretted his decision to use Portland stone for his Nefertiti bust. This is the best carving limestone available in the UK but, as quickly became apparent, it is not easy to work. The fact that London's Whitehall Cenotaph is made from Portland stone gives some idea of its toughness and durability. Starting with a 195kg (430lb) block, it took Frank two months to chip the excess stone away, and it was three months before the block could be lifted onto his workbench. His experience makes it very clear why Thutmose and his men would chose work in the open courtyard, close by the compound gate. No one wants to move a heavy stone block more often than necessary, and even a relatively small block of stone is very heavy. Having chipped away at least three-quarters of it, and generated a significant pile of debris, Frank now has a block measuring 35 × 27 × 59cm (14 × 11 × 23in), which includes 10cm (4in) of base that will eventually be removed from the sculpture. In ancient Egypt, too, all statues started life as a stone block cut slightly larger than the desired end product. The extraction of a soft stone (limestone or sandstone) block from the quarry was a relatively simple procedure as the stone could be cut using copper tools. Hard stone blocks were an entirely different matter, as they were too hard to cut using saws and chisels. Evidence preserved in the Aswan granite quarries indicates that these blocks were separated from the motherrock by teams of men rhythmically bouncing hammer-stone balls of dolerite (an even harder rock) against the surface, to wear it away.

For all sculptors, modern and ancient, planning is the key to success. Frank planned his work by drawing all four sides of the head onto a graticule, and using this as the basis for all measurements. Guidelines were transferred to the block, which was worked evenly all round, leaving the face until last. Thutmose, too, would have covered his block with a network of accurately measured guidelines; these would ensure that the statue did not distort or twist during its cutting. He would then have sketched the image – front, back, profile and top – onto the stone in black ink. Several of the unfinished pieces recovered from Thutmose's workshop show these black guidelines. With the outline in place the stone could be cut away from all surfaces, with the guidelines being reapplied at frequent intervals to keep the statue true. Again, this would be a relatively quick and easy process when working with soft stone, and a time-consuming and difficult one when working with hard stone, which could only be cut using hammer-stones and drills employing a sand abrasive. Whatever the stone, Egyptian statues were rarely cut entirely free of their original block: arms tended to remain close to the body; stone was left in place between the legs and between the arms and the body; and most stone statues were supported by an integral plinth and back pillar. This, combined with the tradition of 'frontality' which dictated that royal and divine subjects always faced straight ahead without any noticeable bending or turning of the head or body, allowed the stone statues to develop a static dignity. Contemporary wooden statues, far lighter, and equipped with jointed shoulders which allowed the arms to extend and hold things, were able to achieve a more active, but perhaps less imposing, royal presence.

Nefertiti has taken a year of Frank's life so far, working an average of half an hour per day, and he still has many hours to go. But he estimates that in a workshop, with experienced craftsmen, appropriate tools and the appropriate quality and quantity of limestone, the stone head could have been created in approximately six weeks. The plaster and paint would then be relatively quick additions to the original; it is the need to create an exact replica which makes this stage so slow in the Gipsformerei. Shaun Greenhalgh is a much faster worker; he reportedly took just three weeks to create his unpainted Amarna princess using modern tools and a very soft stone, but this is not a particularly relevant parallel, as his princess is a very different shape and, crucially, lacks the face that would require delicate modelling. The most surprising thing to come out of Frank's work so far is the fact that, when struck with a hammer, his Nefertiti bust rings with the sound of a slightly muffled bell.

The Popular Queen

Inevitably, the Berlin queen – or for many who saw it in their local museum, Haim's version of the Berlin queen – became the one and only popular version of Nefertiti. Defined by her flat-topped crown, she quickly passed into popular culture as a beautiful, powerful and exotic woman. This version of Nefertiti has for over a century been depicted in novels, plays, films and operas, and has even made an appearance in the BBC's *Doctor Who*. Her image, often reduced to a silhouette, has been used to sell a wide range of luxurious, female-based products, from cosmetics and underwear to holidays. Occasionally it is the bust itself that features in popular culture; a replica Nefertiti bust, for example, plays a key role in Kingsley Amis and Robert Conquest's *The Egyptologists* (1965), and is featured on several versions of the book's cover. Less successfully, a Nefertiti bust is displayed in the Cleopatra Club in Quentin Tarantino's 2013 film *Django Unchained*. The film is set in 1858. Whether or not it actually existed, Nefertiti's personal flat-topped crown has assumed a surprising cultural life of its own. In the 1935 film *The Bride of Frankenstein*, Elsa Lanchester's hair was subjected to a Marcel wave then stretched over a wire frame to create a modern version of Nefertiti's crown: an iconic tall, dark tower with a white lightning bolt on each side. This has evolved into the hairstyle sported by the Lego Bride of Frankenstein today. Lanchester's hairstyle was replicated by Magenta the castle maid, played by Patricia Quinn, in the 1975 film of the *Rocky Horror Show*.[16]

While many have drawn inspiration from the bust, using it to develop their own interpretation of Nefertiti the woman, some artists have regarded it as an object in its own right, and have been happy to isolate it from its original context. These artists may or may not have an understanding of the history underpinning the statue; some may regard that history as irrelevant. They do, however, all share a conviction that the bust should not be allowed to linger in the past; that it has to keep moving forward to survive as a culturally relevant object. This is a theme that has been repeated many times over the past century, with one of the first to express this view to a wide public being Madame Yevonde (Yevonde Middleton), a pioneer of colour photography who in 1938 used the now defunct Vivex colour process to create her still life *Bust of Nefertiti with Flat Iron and Letters*. In her photograph the bust appears an uncompromising, unpainted white, although her lips and cheeks are tinted and both eyes have been drawn in. The arms which hold the vivid yellow flat iron belong to a living woman hidden behind the bust.

Others have continued along this route. In 1993 American artist Fred Wilson created *Grey Area (Brown version)*: five plaster replicas of the Berlin bust placed on high wooden shelves which force the viewer to look up, which the artist painted in various shades of skin tone ranging from oatmeal to dark chocolate.[17] Here the bust represents one of the most copied artworks of ancient civilisation, while the five identical but differently coloured Nefertitis raise questions about the racial identity of the ancient Egyptians. In 2012 German artist Isa Genzken added sunglasses to seven painted Nefertiti replicas exhibited on white painted wooden plinths to create *Nofretete*. Her Nefertiti, an ancient icon of feminine beauty, is used to explore the place of women in art. Also in 2012, Sam Bardaouil and Till

Fellrath of the multidisciplinary cultural platform Art Reoriented created *Tea with Nefertiti: The Making of the Artwork by the Artist, the Museum, and the Public*. This was an exhibition of works by forty mainly contemporary artists displayed alongside works by ancient Egyptian artists. Using the Nefertiti bust as a metaphorical thread, they explored the ways in which exhibitions and artworks create images of other cultures, while examining the way in which a work of art may acquire different meanings when it travels through time and place.

The Neues Museum has always endeavoured to present Nefertiti in new and unexpected contexts. In the Altes Museum she had stood in splendid isolation:

> *Nefertiti was installed in the central hall on the first storey, looking out through the rotunda ... in visual contact with the present. From the balcony, over the flight of stairs, those entering were offered a view that was not difficult to understand pragmatically: directly under Nefertiti in the central hall on the ground floor stood The Praying Boy, his arms raised up to Egypt.*[18]

In the Neues Museum the bust is displayed in the north dome room, where it is approached through three Amarna rooms designed to set Nefertiti in her proper context. The bust sits on a black column protected by a glass case which allows visitors to inspect Nefertiti from all angles while, as the museum's website tells us, allowing the queen herself to participate in the museum experience: 'The gaze of the Sun Queen goes through the rooms of the New Museum right through to the south dome where it meets the statue of the sun-god Helios from Alexandria.' The room is semi-dark, with lighting designed to emphasise the delicate modelling of the queen's face. A bronze bust of James Simon, created by Tina Haim-Wentscher in 1931, is Nefertiti's only neighbour.

We have already seen Little Warsaw's attempt to place Nefertiti's bust in a new, contemporary context, and the controversy that this provoked. In March 2005 the bust became the focus of the temporary exhibition *Hieroglyphs Around Nefertiti*, in the Kulturforum on Matthäikirchplatz. This exhibition, which aimed to trace the legibility of pictorial signs, placed Nefertiti alongside some of the more contemporary artworks in the Berlin collections, including works by Albrecht Dürer, Paul Klee and Max Ernst. Two years later, in 2007, the Italian ambassador curated an exhibition on the theme of Beauty, and chose to place a terracotta head belonging to the Ife culture beside the Nefertiti bust as a reminder of Egypt's African nature. More recently, the entirely conventional exhibition *In the Light of Amarna*, a celebration of the centenary of the bust's discovery, proved to be a huge popular success, attracting over 500,000 visitors to the Neues Museum.

In March 2016 came news of a daring art project: *The Other Nefertiti*. Using cameras strapped to their bodies and concealed by scarves, artists Nora Al-Badri and Jan Nikolai Nelles had visited the Neues Museum and illicitly scanned the bust of Nefertiti. They revealed their project at the 32nd Chaos Communication Congress, an annual conference organised by the Chaos Computer Club, and set up a website with a link to a torrent download, so that anyone with the right computer equipment might have instant, free access to the bust: 'With the data leak as part of this counter narrative we want to activate the artefact, to inspire a critical re-assessment of today's conditions and to overcome the colonial notion of possession in Germany.'[19]

The project was designed as a direct response to the Neues Museum's refusal to make its own scans public while continuing to profit from the sale of replicas in the museum shop. The artists claimed to have used their data to create their own 3D printed polymer resin replica, which they were proposing to exhibit at the

Something Else, Off Biennale Cairo initiative, before donating it to the American University in Cairo.

The free scan supplied by *The Other Nefertiti* provoked intense media coverage, and the artists earned praise for their attempts to 'repatriate' Nefertiti.[20] It is impossible to know how many replicas were created from their data, but one is currently being displayed free of charge to the general public in the Hattiesburg Public Library, Mississippi. This replica was created by Mark Landis working in collaboration with the group known as Southern Artists, Forgers and Hackers.[21] Taking over 150 hours to create on a 3D printer, the Landis Nefertiti was printed in three pieces at a 150-micron resolution out of a hybrid filament of wood particles and polylactic acid plastic. Each piece of the printed sculpture was then inspected, hand aligned and glued together. Once dry, the seams were filled in and the sculpture sanded to provide a smooth surface for painting. Landis then hand painted the bust to match photographs of the original. The Landis bust was not simply created as an easy means of obtaining a replica Nefertiti. Southern Artists, Forgers and Hackers were inspired by the Pirate Party's platform of defending the free flow of ideas, knowledge and culture.[22] They believe that 3D printing can be used to decentralise notable works of sculpture, with *The Other Nefertiti* project presenting a perfect opportunity for them to realise a reproduction. As 'Michelle', one of the artists, has commented: 'the Nefertiti Bust is absolutely the most important object currently available to 3D print from an artistic perspective. It is also delightfully accessible and easy for anyone to print on a small scale.'[23]

Despite the undeniable fact that *The Other Nefertiti* made a 3D Nefertiti scan widely available to the general public, the project is unconvincing. Al-Badri and Nelles claim to have used a scanner of such low resolution and accuracy that it would quite simply have been incapable of creating a model as accurate as that subsequently supplied on their website. Cosmo Wenman, a specialist in digitally preserving and sharing scans of museum sculptures, has concluded that the scan they provide was actually obtained either by scanning a high-quality replica or, as seems more likely to him, by using an unpublished scan created for the Neues Museum by TrigonArt in 2008.[24] Wenman's deduction is supported by an interview given by Nelles, in which he explains that the artists themselves were only a part of the project. They were given the recording equipment by an unnamed partner, who subsequently 'processed' the data and produced the 3D model.[25] The unknown partner has since vanished, leaving Al-Badri and Nelles to explain their impossible scans. In August 2016 Wenman sent a formal legal request to the Neues Museum requesting copies of their data from the 3D scan of the Nefertiti bust citing Berlin State and Federal German freedom of information laws. This request was turned down on the grounds of commercial sensitivity.

8

LOOKING FOR NEFERTITI

Let a tomb be made for me in the eastern mountain [of Akhenaten]. Let my burial be made in it, in the millions of jubilees which the Aten, my father, decreed for me. Let the burial for the King's Great Wife Nefertiti be made in it, in the millions of years which the Aten, my father, decreed for her. (And) let the burial of the King's Daughter Meritaten [be made] in it, in these millions of years.[1]

Amarna Boundary Stelae inscription

Although we have many images of Nefertiti, in both two and three dimensions, few of these are dated. One tomb scene, however, places Nefertiti firmly at the heart of the royal family towards the end of Akhenaten's reign. On the wall of the tomb decorated for Meryre II we can see the entire royal family – Akhenaten, Nefertiti and all six daughters – enjoying a festival or *durbar* that Meryre helpfully dates to regnal year 12.[2] Our next sighting of the queen is a far sadder scene; the walls of the royal tomb show Akhenaten,

Nefertiti and their three eldest surviving daughters mourning the death of Princess Meketaten. As we saw Meketaten apparently alive and well at the regnal year 12 celebrations we can be reasonably confident that she died after the festival. We cannot be entirely sure of this, though; the Amarna artists had been happy to depict Amenhotep III dining with Queen Tiy in Huya's tomb, even though he was long dead when the tomb was decorated. As Barry Kemp reminds us: 'Tomb pictures are not photographs. They are compositions intended to reflect, in part, something suited to eternal contemplation.'[3]

Our final mention of Nefertiti dates to Akhenaten's sixteenth regnal year. A barely legible graffito carved in the Dayr Abu Hinnis quarry, 10km to the north of Amarna, on the '15th day of the 3rd month of inundation, year 16', specifically mentions the 'Great King's Wife, his beloved, mistress of the Two Lands, Neferneferuaten Nefertiti'.[4] It seems that Nefertiti was alive and performing her normal consort's duties shortly before Akhenaten's death. His last recorded date comes from a wine jar labelled 'year 17, second month of the inundation'.

On the basis of this evidence, it seems that Nefertiti either survived her husband or predeceased him by a year or less. If she survived Akhenaten, we would expect her to have handed over her role to her successor as queen consort, and to have faded somewhat from our view. Depending on where and when she died, she might then have been interred in the Amarna royal tomb. If she predeceased Akhenaten, we would have expected him to have stuck with his original plan, and to have buried his wife in or very near the royal tomb.[5] The first visitors to Amarna had been happy to accept that this is what happened. It was a common enough tragedy; the thin and fragile queen, who looked ill to the point of consumption, had simply succumbed to illness:

Nofre-ti-tai-Aten seems to have ultimately died of decline, for there is a very sad sculpture in which she appears in the last stage of it, her cheeks hollow, her once beautiful face shrunken to nothing, and death obviously not far off. It is to be found in the northern group of tombs.[6]

Unfortunately the royal tomb is less informative on this subject than we might have hoped. At the very least, it was emptied by Tutankhamen, whom we must assume moved all the important and valuable burials and grave goods to Thebes, and was thoroughly ransacked by locals sometime during the early 1880s, before its rediscovery was reported to the authorities. It is likely to have been looted many times between these two known events. This vandalism makes it difficult for us to assess who was, and who was not, buried there. We can only state that there is no mention of Nefertiti's death either in the royal tomb or elsewhere, and the only evidence for her interment at Amarna is provided by a broken shabti whose separate pieces are now housed in the Louvre and Brooklyn Museum, and whose inscription has been reconstructed by Christian Loeben to read:

The Heiress, high and mighty in the palace, one trusted of the King of Upper and Lower Egypt Neferkheperure Waenre, the Son of Re [Akhenaten], Great in his lifetime, The Chief Wife of the King, Neferneferuaten-Nefertiti, Living for ever and ever.[7]

This shabti, like the regnal year 16 graffito, implies that Nefertiti died a queen consort.

However, the regnal year 16 graffito was only discovered and published in 2012. For many years prior to its publication, Egyptologists had accepted that Nefertiti vanished soon after the death of Meketaten, probably in year 13, leaving a four-year Nefertiti-less gap at the end of Akhenaten's reign. This should not have been a problem. Egyptian history is riddled with vanishing queens; invariably, this means that they have died. However, there has been a general reluctance to accept that a queen as prominent as Nefertiti could have died without Akhenaten informing us of her demise, and this has led to a lot of speculation about what many have seen as her inexplicable disappearance. These theories linger in the literature to confuse our thinking about the end of the Amarna Period. They may be divided into two categories:

(1) Nefertiti was banished from court during the latter part of her husband's reign, making it impossible for us to see her.

(2) Nefertiti changed her name two or three times during the later stages of her life, making it impossible for us to see her.

The Lady Vanishes

The suggestion that Nefertiti was banished from court can be immediately dismissed. This was based on the observation that, at the Amarna temple known as Maru-Aten, Meritaten's name was inscribed over the name of another woman. Under the erroneous impression that Nefertiti had been ruthlessly erased, John Pendlebury suggested that there had been a quarrel that left Nefertiti, the Aten's most faithful disciple, confined to one of the Amarna palaces.[8] Norman de Garis Davies suggested the opposite: that Nefertiti had been happy to deny the Aten, and that she had been banished to allow Akhenaten to marry Meritaten and father a son.[9] We now know that the erased name belonged to Kiya, making the various Nefertiti disgrace and banishment theories redundant.

The suggestion that Nefertiti changed her role, and in so doing became invisible to us, deserves more consideration. In the 1970s philologist John Harris wrote a series of articles that led to the development of the theory that Nefertiti transformed herself into a female king to rule alongside Akhenaten as a co-regent.[10] After Akhenaten's death, she may even have ruled Egypt either as a solo king or as a regent, before Tutankhamen came to the throne.[11] This theory can be supported by a certain amount of indirect linguistic and artistic evidence but, as is so often the case with the Amarna Period, this is far from conclusive. Much of this evidence comes from Tutankhamen's tomb, which includes a surprising number of grave goods recycled from Amarna burials. Included amongst these is, to take just one example of the 'evidence' that can be read two ways, a gilded statuette which depicts a king dressed in a kilt and white crown, standing on the back of a leopard. The figure shows what have been described as 'prominent breasts and low hips'.[12] Some experts have interpreted this as a statuette originally made for a woman: a piece created for King Nefertiti's burial, repurposed by Tutankhamen, perhaps? Others have simply seen it as an Amarna-style young Tutankhamen.

The situation is complicated by the introduction of two new characters who appear, seemingly from nowhere, at the heart of the nuclear royal family during the final years of Akhenaten's reign. There is no doubt that 'Ankhkheperure Neferneferuaten' and 'Ankhkheperure Smenkhkare' existed. Their names are attested in several Amarna contexts, but we cannot be certain who they were, or what role they played in the succession.[13] Many believe that these could both be Nefertiti, changing her name as she advanced from co-ruler (Ankhkheperure Neferneferuaten) to solo king (Ankhkheperure Smenkhkare). However, this would have been an unprecedented move followed by a highly unusual move. No consort had ever become an official co-ruler alongside her husband and, although two women (the Twelfth Dynasty Sobeknofru and

Eighteenth Dynasty Hatshepsut) had ruled Egypt as a female kings, both had royal fathers.

We know that Tutankhamen ultimately succeeded Akhenaten, but we don't know what happened in the short gap between Akhenaten's death and Tutankhamen's coronation. Given the lack of concrete information about Akhenaten's immediate successor, it would be useful to stop focusing on the minutiae of name development and unlabelled sketches, and to spend a moment looking at the bigger picture. Is there any evidence to support the supposition that Nefertiti was an especially powerful consort allocated a unique role? If we draw a direct comparison between Nefertiti and Tiy, the answer has to be no. Each queen features prominently in her husband's reign. Each can appear at the same size as her husband; each can also appear unnaturally small. Tiy is worshipped in Nubia; Nefertiti is worshipped at Amarna. Tiy is mentioned in diplomatic correspondence and despatches her enemies as a sphinx; Nefertiti conducts religious rites in Thebes and smites her enemies with a weapon. Both women are living solar goddesses, each wears Tefnut's distinctive crown, and each is linked to Hathor.

While absence of evidence can never be considered evidence of absence, we don't have a single image or fragment of text to prove that Nefertiti was ever considered to be Akhenaten's equal, or co-regent. In any scene shared by the two, it is Nefertiti who is the minor, supporting figure. It is true that the Berlin Museum scene of the royal family sitting beneath the Aten shows Nefertiti sitting on a more highly decorated seat than her husband, but if we look again at the scene in the tomb of Kheruef which shows Tiy depicted as a sphinx, we see exactly the same thing. Tiy's seat is more decorated than Amenhotep's, leading us to assume that this should not be read as an unusual sign of authority.[14] Nefertiti helps and encourages her husband's actions, but she is a cipher who will not disturb *maat* by contributing any unexpected individuality. It is only when her husband is absent that she is able to perform actions and express individuality appropriate to her role. This visual evidence confirms what we might have expected from the complete absence of textual references to Nefertiti as co-regent. Her occasional regal regalia, her prominent religious duties and her appearance in the smiting scenes, are very much a continuation of the elevation of the queenship that was started during the reign of Amenhotep III. Yet, many sources include Nefertiti amongst the list of Egypt's kings without any qualification or hint that it is a far from a proven theory.[15]

If Nefertiti is not Neferneferuaten and Smenkhkare, who are they? There are no named depictions of 'Neferneferuaten', but a graffito scribbled in the Theban tomb of Pere refers to regnal year 3 of 'Ankhkheperure beloved of the Aten, the son of Re: Neferneferuaten beloved of Waenre [Akhenaten]'.[16] In 1998 a close examination of Neferneferuaten's cartouche led linguist Marc Gabolde to recognise that it occasionally includes the epithet 'effective for her husband'.[17] Neferneferuaten then was female. If we are looking for a powerful female operating at the end of the Amarna Period, we should probably be paying more attention to Nefertiti's eldest daughter Meritaten, a woman of royal birth with a far greater claim to the throne than her mother.[18] It would make perfect sense for Meritaten to serve first as King's Daughter (to Akhenaten) then as king's wife (to the short-lived Smenkhkare) then finally as act as regent to the young Tutankhamen, who inherited this throne at just eight years of age and who would have needed guidance.

To find evidence for the elusive Smenkhkare, we need to return to the tomb of Meryre II. We have already seen the royal family enjoying the regnal year 12 festival on the east wall. On the damaged north wall we see an incomplete, unpainted scene.[19] A typical Amarna-style king and queen stand beneath the rays of the Aten to reward the faithful Meryre. They could well be Akhenaten and Nefertiti, but the names recorded in the cartouches are those of the

'King of Upper and Lower Egypt, Ankhkheperure son of Re, Smenkhkare-djeserkheperu' and the 'King's Great Wife Meritaten'. Unfortunately, the king's cartouche was removed by thieves before Davies recorded the tomb; fortunately, it had been copied by Lepsius and preserved in the form of a squeeze (an impression made by pressing damp, mouldable paper or plaster into the relief) by Egyptologist Nestor L'Hôte, and Davies was happy to accept his copies. The scene is undated; it is likely that it was started after the year 12 scene, but just how long after we do not know. If we are to interpret this evidence literally, and there seems to be no reason not to, we can deduce that Akhenaten died while Meryre's tomb was being decorated, forcing the artists to adapt a scene of Akhenaten and Nefertiti so that it became the new king Smenkhkare and his wife Meritaten. This suggests that Smenkhkare was in the direct line of succession; a son born to Akhenaten and one of his many wives, married to his sister or half sister.

Smenkhkare seems to have enjoyed a very brief reign at Amarna, leaving few traces in the archaeological record. His highest regnal year date is a wine label dated to year 1. We may, however, have his remains. On 6 January 1907 a mission led by British Egyptologist Edward Ayrton and financed by American lawyer-turned-Egyptologist Theodore Davis discovered an unfinished, single-chambered tomb (KV 55) not far from Tutankhamen's own as yet undiscovered tomb in the Valley of the Kings.[20] KV 55 had been a cache or workshop tomb, used during Tutankhamen's reign as temporary accommodation for the bodies and grave goods rescued from the Amarna royal burials. Here the royal burials had been restored, and in many cases their grave goods reworked and reassigned, before being allocated to more appropriate tombs in the valley. As a result, KV 55 has yielded the remains of many Amarna burials, jumbled together. Amongst these was an elaborate anthropoid coffin which had been created for an elite woman then modified for use by an unknown royal man. The coffin held a rotting mummy which survives today as a skeleton in the Cairo Museum.

Davies believed that he had discovered the remains of Queen Tiy, but all who have since examined the bones have agreed that they belong to a man closely related to Tutankhamen. We know that Tutankhamen sealed KV 55, and we know that he died at approximately eighteen years of age. As he could not have buried an adult son, the KV 55 skeleton is likely to be either his father or his brother. The older the remains, the more likely they are to be his father (Akhenaten?); the younger they are, the more likely they are to be his brother (Smenkhkare?). Unfortunately, as so often happens in Egyptology, the experts are divided on this matter. Grafton Elliot Smith, anatomist at the Cairo Medical School, initially estimated an age at death of twenty-five or twenty-six years, then extended it to allow for the possibility that this could be Akhenaten.[21] Douglas Derry, Professor of Anatomy at the Cairo Medical School, felt that the skeleton could have been no more than twenty-five years old.[22] Ronald Harrison, Professor of Anatomy at Liverpool University, and independent anatomist Joyce Filer are in close agreement: the KV 55 male died at less than twenty-five years of age, probably in his twentieth year.[23] However, James Harris, Chairman of the Department of Orthodontics at the University of Michigan, has suggested an age of thirty to thirty-five,[24] while the most recent analysis, conducted by the Supreme Council of Antiquities, gave estimates ranging from between thirty-five and forty-five years to a more improbable sixty.[25] Citing DNA evidence, the Egyptian team have identified the KV 55 male as both the father of Tutankhamen and a son of Amenhotep III and Tiy: they conclude that he is 'most probably Akhenaten'. This identification has provoked widespread debate. Mummy DNA analysis is still in its infancy, and poses many problems for the Egyptologist, with both contamination and heat damage being significant limiting factors.

Many, the present author included, would still identify the KV 55 mummy as the relatively young Smenkhkare, an older brother of Tutankhamen.

Finding Nefertiti

The Eighteenth Dynasty has provided us with many missing queens and many unidentified female mummies. Egyptologists have been struggling for years to match the two. The quest to find Nefertiti has been a particularly compelling one, which has attracted the attention of the world's press.

Wherever she was originally buried, there is a strong possibility that Nefertiti was eventually interred on the Theban west bank. It therefore makes good sense to search for her body there. Independent scholar Marianne Luban was the first to propose, on the grounds of skull shape, bone structure, the shaven head and evidence of ear piercing, that a mummy known as the 'Younger Lady', discovered as part of a secondary burial in a side chamber in the tomb of Amenhotep II (KV 35), may be Nefertiti.[26] But when a team from York University carried out a non-invasive examination of this mummy, and came to the same conclusion, the situation was complicated by the publication of a report from the Egyptian Supreme Council of Antiquities, which stated that DNA testing had revealed the Younger Lady to be male.[27] More recent testing has confirmed that the mummy is, indeed, female, while DNA analysis performed by the Supreme Council of Antiquities research team has suggested, confusingly, that the Younger Lady was both Tutankhamen's mother and a previously unknown sister of the KV 55 male.[28] Mummy DNA evidence is, however, as we have already noted, notoriously unreliable. If we look at her teeth, the Younger Lady would seem to be too young to be Nefertiti as the incomplete root formation of the wisdom teeth suggests an age of fifteen to sixteen years.[29] Could we have Meritaten, or even the relocated Meketaten, here?

As I write, Egypt's Supreme Council of Antiquities is still assessing the suggestion made by British Egyptologist Nicolas Reeves, that the plaster walls of Tutankhamen's burial chamber conceal two doorways, one leading to a storage room and one to the undisturbed burial of Nefertiti.[30] Reeves's theory is based on the identification of irregularities beneath the painted plaster, spotted when the art-replication specialists Factum Arte took a detailed series of photographs and scans as a preliminary to creating an exact replica of the tomb for tourists to visit. The problem is that any direct investigation of the surface below the plaster is likely to cause irreparable damage to the tomb.

Tutankhamen's tomb (KV 62) is certainly a curious one, being unexpectedly small and inconveniently placed in the valley floor. The accepted explanation for this cramped burial is that Tutankhamen died before his own tomb was complete, forcing his successor, the elderly courtier Ay, to bury him in the tomb that he had been preparing for himself. However, Tutankhamen's builders would have had at least six years to construct a suitably regal tomb, and that should have been plenty of time. It seems far more likely that Ay, inheriting the throne as an elderly man, made a strategic swap. Four years after Tutankhamen was buried in his unsuitable tomb, Ay himself was buried in a spacious yet unfinished tomb (KV 23), close by the tomb of Tutankhamen's illustrious ancestor, Amenhotep III (KV 22).

Reeves has put forward the intriguing alternative suggestion that the tomb is small because it is, in fact, only the entrance area of a far larger tomb, built to house the burial of Nefertiti following her reign as the female pharaoh known as Ankhkheperure Smenkhkare-djeserkheperu. This would be an extraordinary development. While it is not unlikely that Tutankhamen's private tomb was incomplete when it was hastily converted into a royal tomb – the neighbouring, contemporary tomb KV 55 was incomplete when it was pressed into service as a workshop, and its 'burial chamber' shows the evidence of an unfinished doorway – it would be completely without precedent to find an intact royal burial hidden behind its walls. Does Nefertiti still have the power to surprise us?

NOTES

Introduction Seeking Nefertiti

1. Baikie (1929: 3), writing not long after the public unveiling of the Berlin
    bust of Nefertiti, provides the introductory chapter for *Great Ones of Ancient
    Egypt*: a series of brief biographies accompanied by modern portraits by
    Winifed Brunton. The 'Great Ones' selected for portraits include
    Amenhotep III, Tiy, Smenkhkare, Tutankhamen and Ankhesenamen, but
    neither Akhenaten nor Nefertiti.
2. Tyldesley (1998).
3. Carter and Mace (1923). For a discussion of the discovery of Tutankhamen's
    tomb, and the outbreak of 'Tut-mania' see Tyldesley (2012).

Background to the Amarna Age

1. Murray (1949: 54).
2. Ägyptisches Museum Berlin: ÄM 21300.
3. Readers interested in the complex relationship between Akhenaten, the Aten
    and Amarna, may like to consult Dodson (2009, 2014), Kemp (2012),
    Redford (1984), Reeves (2001) or Tyldesley (1998). Each of these authorities

uses the same evidence to tell the same story in a different way. Proof, if proof were needed, that there is as yet no universally acknowledged version of Egyptian history.

4. Based on the chronology suggested by Shaw (2000: 481).

5. Figure suggested by Kemp (2012: 17). Kemp adds that 'maybe twice that number' followed Akhenaten to Amarna.

PART I Creating Nefertiti

1. March Phillipps (1911: 43).

2. Baikie (1926: 292–3).

1 Thutmose

1. Davies (1903–8, III: 14).

2. Ägyptisches Museum Berlin: ÄM 21193. To read about the identification of the blinker, see Krauss (1983).

3. I am grateful to Dr Pauline Norris for sharing this insight.

4. The tomb of Khaemhat (TT 57) remains unpublished. The horses and their blinkers can be seen in Griffith Institute squeeze 4.27: http://www.griffith. ox.ac.uk/gri/4gisquee.html.

5. The incomplete Amarna tomb of Ay (Amarna Tomb 25), for example, shows Ay and his wife Tey receiving gold necklaces from the royal family. Davies (1903–8, VI: Plate XXIX).

6. The original names and numbers for the Amarna houses, streets and suburbs are now lost. The names and numbers used here are those given by the archaeologists who have worked at the site.

7. Thutmose's extensive compound is designated P47.1–3; his villa is P47.2. Seyfried (2012) provides a series of helpful plans.

8. Ägyptisches Museum Berlin: ÄM 29881.

9. This house is designated P47.4.

10. See, for example, Carter (1933: Plates II, XII and XIII).

11. Petrie (1894: 30). Hodgkinson (2013) provides a valuable analysis of the evidence for production and socio-economics in New Kingdom royal cities, with a focus on Amarna.

12. For example, Shaw (2004: 18) highlights a group of houses arranged around a courtyard (P49.3–6): although Borchardt's team excavated the houses, it was only during the 1987 excavation season that large quantities of basalt fragments were found in the courtyard. This would appear to be yet another sculptor's workshop.

13. Many of these fragments were excavated by John Pendlebury in the 1930s; he reburied them to conserve them when it became clear that no museum was interested in acquiring them. Today they are being re-excavated by the current Amarna team.

14. Amarna Tomb 1. Davies (1903–8, III: Plates X and XI).

15. Today they are displayed in Cairo and Luxor Museums.

16. Petrie (1894: 18).

17. Petrie (1932: 142).

18. Harrell (2014: 9).

19. This house is designated R43.2. For a discussion of this discovery, see Hill (2011).

20. For further information about smiting scenes see Hall (1986). It seems unlikely that the stone statue(s) which originally rested in this wooden shrine would have depicted a smiting scene, as this theme did not appear in three-dimensional stone until the Nineteenth Dynasty.

21. Reeves (1990: 128–32).

22. For a full translation of this stela with commentary, consult Lichtheim (1976: 43–8).

23. Many of the Sekhmet statues were discovered out of their original context, having been moved in antiquity to the Mut Temple, which is part of the Karnak Temple complex of Amen. Examples may be found in many Western museums, with more than thirty being housed in the collections of the British Museum.

24. The name and appearance of the Aten is discussed in more detail in Goldwasser (2010).

25. Davies (1903–8, II: 24 and Plate XIX) illustrates and describes the *benben* in the tomb of the 'chief servitor of the Aten in the temple of the Aten in Akhetaten' Panehsy (Amarna Tomb 6). Various excavators have discovered

fragments of red quartzite and 'black granite' (possibly diorite) within the Great Temple; these may represent the remains of the *benben* and its associated statue.

26. Ägyptisches Museum Berlin: ÄM 37391.
27. Ägyptisches Museum Berlin: ÄM 34701.
28. Bennet (1939). Part of a duplicate text was discovered in the temple of Montu at Karnak. Both are now in the collections of the Cairo Museum (JE 41504 and 41565).
29. House T34.1: Willems (1998: 240).
30. The Akhenaten and Nefertiti busts are now in the Ägyptisches Museum Berlin: ÄM 21360 and 21300. An additional plaster head was discovered in R14.
31. Ägyptisches Museum Berlin: limestone statue ÄM 21263; plaster model ÄM 21349; limestone head ÄM 21352.
32. Petrie (1894: 40). Cairo Museum: JE 753.
33. R. H. Hall, Keeper of Egyptian and Assyrian Antiquities in the British Museum, writing for the *Illustrated London News*, 19 March 1927.
34. Roeder (1941: 154–60).
35. Wildung (2012: 36).
36. Thutmose's tomb is numbered Bubasteion 1.19, Maya's tomb Bubasteion 1.20. They were discovered on the same day, by the Mission Archéologique Française du Bubasteion directed by Alain Zivie. Zivie (2013).
37. Discussed in Černý (2001: 35–40).
38. Amarna Tomb 8. Murnane (1995: 187).

2 Chief of Works

1. Gombrich (1972 [1950]: 4).
2. We may not know the names of the nineteenth- and twentieth-century sculptors whose works surround us on the streets of London, Paris or, in my case, Bolton, but this is because we tend not to notice public art; the name of the artist will be available if we wish to seek it out.
3. See, for example, Duncan (1995: 7).
4. Baines (1994: 67). Baines concludes his discussion by saying that 'Egyptian art is a typically inward-looking and almost self-sustaining product of a

professional group. It is no less "art" for the wide range of functions and purposes it fulfilled.'

5. Davies (1903–8, III: 13–14 and Plate XVIII). Huya, whose many and varied titles included 'superintendent of the royal harem, superintendent of the treasury, steward in the house of the King's Mother', was the steward of Queen Tiy. As such, he was responsible for all the craftsmen who worked for the dowager queen.

6. Hatiay's stela is now housed in Leiden Museum: Leiden VI. It has been discussed by several authorities including Kruchten (1992) and Willems (1998).

7. Van Dijk (1995: 29–30). I have amended his translation slightly.

8. The Memphite Theology, as recorded on the Shabaka Stone, British Museum: EA 498. Translation after Lichtheim (1973: 54).

9. Tyldesley (1996: 194).

10. Murnane (1995: 128–9).

11. Krauss (1986). Ägyptisches Museum: ÄM 31009. The provenance of this piece is unknown.

12. Murnane (1995: 192).

13. Smith (2012: 70–73 and Plate LXII).

14. For example, Ramesses II was never depicted as the ninety-year-old king that he became; Tutankhamen was approximately eighteen when he died, yet some of his statuary gives him the maturity of a middle-aged man; the mummies of the Tuthmoside kings and queens betray their pronounced incisors; the Twelfth Dynasty female king Sobeknofru wore a dress and a kilt simultaneously in an attempt to conform to the male and female dress codes.

15. Kozloff and Bryan (1992: 127).

16. Robins (1986: 43–52).

17. Schäfer (1919); discussed in Baines (1985).

18. Winckelmann (1764: 191–2).

19. Preziosi (2009: 14).

20. Moser (2006: 34), describes the early British Museum presentation of its Egyptology collection as 'objects that were designed to surprise and entertain, as opposed to those that were intended to inform and enlighten'.

21. Assmann (1996: 56).

22. British Museum: EA 15. Patmore (1826: 35).

23. Ashmolean Museum: 1894/105e.

24. Ashmolean Museum: 1894/105d and 105e. Petrie (1932: 153).

25. The stylistic evolution of Amenhotep's image, with particular reference to the Luxor Temple, is discussed by Johnson (1998: 80–94).

26. British Museum: EA7399.

27. Weigall (1922: 44).

3 Taught by the King

1. Remarks on Hamilton's Aegyptica, *Edinburgh Review* (1811) 36: 436. Discussed in Moser (2006: 89).

2. Louvre Museum: N.831(AF.109). The figure is made out of a curious yellow stone, variously described as limestone or steatite. It entered the Louvre in 1826 as part of the Salt collection, provenance unknown.

3. Discussed by Johnson (1998: 91), who cites as an example Ägyptisches Museum Berlin: ÄM 2072.

4. Cairo Museum: JE 55938.

5. Discussed in more detail in Tyldesley (2010: 37–51).

6. Lepsius (1849–58).

7. Krauss (1995) and Silverman et al. (2006: 185) summarise the various explanations for Akhenaten's appearance.

8. Wilkinson (1847: 306–7).

9. Petrie (1894: 39): discussed in Challis (2013: 155–7). Petrie was greatly influenced by the eugenic ideas of Francis Galton, and supported him in his anthropometric data gathering.

10. Petrie (1894: 40).

11. A theory first suggested by Perrot and Chipiez (1883: 244).

12. Weigall (1922: 51–2).

13. *Punch*, 14 February 1923.

14. Arnold (1996: 17).

15. Montserrat (2000: 48).

16. Figures given in the *Independent*, 3 August 2000. Discussed in Tyldesley (2012: 110–11).

17. Arnold (2012: 147). In a highly unscientific experiment I have been asking my students for many years what they think of Akhenaten's extreme

appearance. While some find him disturbing, many find that his face has a compelling sexuality.

18. Gardiner (1961: 214).
19. Aldred (1973: 48–66).
20. Baikie (1917: 178).
21. Baikie (1926: 243).
22. 'Marriage scarab' published by Amenhotep III. Blankenberg-Van Delden (1969: 16).
23. The identification of Tey as Nefertiti's nurse is supported by a relief fragment in the Louvre, which seems to show a woman sitting on the knee of her nurse. The nurse wears a golden necklace, and has one breast exposed. For the suggestion that the two women could be Tey and Nefertiti see Desroches-Noblecourt (1978) for the suggestion that they could be Nefertiti and Meritaten see Arnold (1996: 91–3).
24. Borchardt (1905).
25. Parennefer would soon be required to move to Amarna, where he would be granted a second rock-cut tomb (Tomb 7). As his Amarna tomb has no burial shaft it seems likely that he outlived Akhenaten and returned to Thebes, where he was eventually buried in his original tomb (TT 188). See Davies (1923: 136–45).
26. TT 55. Davies (1941: Plate XXXIII). Ramose disappears from our view when the court moves to Amarna, and it may be that he has already died.
27. Discussed in Williamson (2015).
28. Tyldesley (1996: 89).
29. Discussed in Arnold (1996: 38ff).
30. Assmann (1996: 68).
31. Discussed in O'Connor (2001).
32. Krauss (1995: 749).
33. For a summary of the lives of Egypt's Eighteenth Dynasty queen consorts, see Tyldesley (2006: 86–141).
34. Amarna Letter EA 26. For a translation of the Amarna Letters see Moran (1992).
35. TT 192. Oriental Institute (1980: Plate 46).
36. TT 192. Oriental Institute (1980: Plate 47).
37. Metropolitan Museum of Art: 26.7.1342. There have been suggestions that this bracelet plaque may not be authentic.

4 The Beautiful Woman

1. Baikie (1926: 293).
2. Aakheperure, pers. comm., 2014.
3. For a discussion of this crown see Samson (1973) and Green (1992).
4. Ertman (1976). Nefertiti's cap crown was blue with a yellow band; versions worn during the Nineteenth and Twentieth Dynasties were yellow and covered in discs or circles.
5. Davies (1903–8, II: Plate VIII).
6. The only woman previously known to have worn the *atef* was Hatshepsut, in her role as a female king. It has been suggested that we may have a second representation of Nefertiti wearing this crown in the tomb of Ay: Ertman (1992).
7. Just one example of a perfume cone has been tentatively identified in a burial in the Amarna cemetery: Kemp and Stevens (2010: 10).
8. Louvre Museum: E11076.
9. Quoted in Seyfried (2012: 181). Borchardt's excavation diary for 1912/13 is preserved in the archive of the Berlin Egyptian Museum and Papyrus Collection, and has been published by Seyfried (2011).
10. Arnold (1996: 65).
11. Seyfried (2012: 183).
12. Discussed in Millet (1981). The mastaba tomb took the form of a subterranean burial chamber accessed via a burial shaft and topped by a rectangular stone superstructure known today as a mastaba.
13. The curious circumstances surrounding the discovery of this head are discussed in Tyldesley (2012: 256). Cairo Museum: Carter object number 8.
14. Quoted in the *Illustrated London News*, 17 February 1923: 16. Cairo Museum: Carter object number 116.
15. Discussed in Hoving (1978: 186–7). The quotation is taken from A. H. Bradstreet, who covered the Tutankhamen discovery for both the *Morning Post* and the *New York Times*. Due to an exclusive deal signed with *The Times*, journalists from other newspapers were unable to enter the tomb or make a proper examination of the grave goods; in consequence, their reports tend to be imaginative rather than fact-based.
16. Carter and Mace (1923: 120). The quotation is taken from the *Manchester Guardian*, 27 January 1923.

17. Discussed in Phillips (2004). Thutmose is occasionally credited with being the inventor of the composite statue, but see Thompson (2012: 164).

18. Cairo Museum: JE 59286 (Nefertiti head); ÄM 20494 and 20495 (arm and hands).

19. Ägyptisches Museum Berlin: ÄM 21220.

20. Ägyptisches Museum Berlin: ÄM 21834 (head) and 17852 (headdress).

21. Petrányi (2003).

22. Dietrich Wildung quoted in Eakin (2003).

23. Quoted in Urice (2006: 164).

24. Baines (2007: 264).

25. Discussed by Ashton (2004).

26. Discussed with useful references in Exell (2008).

27. Wildung (2012: 29).

28. Huppertz et al. (2009). The results of the two scans were compared, in an attempt to evaluate damage progression. See Illerhaus et al. (2009).

29. *Independent*, 31 March 2009; *National Geographic*, 30 March 2009; author Michelle Moran, quoted in the *Guardian*, 15 August 2015.

30. Discussed in Sweeney (2004).

31. Ägyptisches Museum Berlin: ÄM 21263. The statuette was found in fragments, and has been almost entirely reconstructed.

32. Wildung (2012: 29). Drooping breasts are often regarded as a signifier of old age, although they can also indicate prolonged breast feeding.

33. Website of the Non Surgical Clinic accessed December 2016. The Nofretete Klinik in Bonn displays a replica bust in its reception area, and has held occasional forums dedicated to the study of Nefertiti in ancient and popular culture.

34. Nileen Namita has received a large amount of coverage in the popular press; see, for example, 'Meet the mother who took her daughter out of top girls' public school because she's spent the fees on plastic surgery', written by Alison Smith Squire for *Mail Online*, 21 March 2011. Namita is not alone in thinking that Nefertiti has been reincarnated; a quick trawl of the internet reveals a wide range of beautiful but tragic women, including Cleopatra, Marie Antoinette, Isadora Duncan, Marilyn Monroe and Princess Diana, who have each been identified, by others, with Nefertiti.

35. Robin Snell, pers. comm., 2016.

36. See, for example, the brightly painted cast of the Peplos Kore in the Museum of Classical Archaeology, Cambridge. She wears a bright red dress decorated with green, white and blue motifs, and has olive skin and red-brown hair. The museum's website tells us that one shocked visitor left the comment 'Didn't like the painted woman …' in the official Visitors' Book. www.classics.cam.ac.uk/museum/collections/peplos-kore.
37. Baines (2007: 245–7).
38. TT 100. Davies (1943: Plate LX).
39. For an introduction to Afrocentric history, see Bernal (1987). See also Lefkowitz and Rogers (1996). Monserrat (2000: 116–23) has highlighted the importance of Akhenaten and his family in Afrocentric history.
40. The New Kingdom mummy known as the 'Younger Lady' (KV 335YL) has a shaven head; this seems to have led to the mummy initially being identified as a man, and to its occasional identification as Nefertiti.
41. For the history of the Nubian wig see Aldred (1957) and Eaton-Krauss (1981). For a discussion of the relationship between hairstyle and social identity see Robins (1999).
42. Paglia (1990: 68).
43. McGuiness (2015: 1).
44. Baikie (1926: 242–3).
45. Reeves (2001: 160).
46. Perrett (2010).
47. Huppertz et al. (2009: 239).
48. Krauss (1991a).
49. Borchardt (1923: 33).
50. Wildung (2012: 22).
51. Borchardt (1923), quoted by Urice (2006: 139) after Krauss (1987: 87).
52. Simon cited by Seyfried (2012: 186 n. 49).
53. Vandenberg (1978).
54. Weigall (1927).
55. *The Sphere*, 4 February 1928: 173.
56. *The Evening Chronicle*, 10 July 1939.

5 The Colourful Queen

1. Edgeworth (2007: 98).
2. Under James Simon's prudent management, Simon Brothers achieved an annual turnover of 50,000,000 Reichsmarks, and an annual profit of 6,000,000 Reichsmarks. Figures quoted by Tony Paterson, *Independent*, 4 December 2012.
3. Roughly the equivalent of €300,000 today; figures suggested by Matthes (2007).
4. Krauss (2008: 47).
5. Borchardt (1923), quoted by Urice (2006: 139) after Krauss (1987: 87).
6. Quoted and discussed by Wildung (2012: 15); Wilhelm (2016: 22).
7. Quoted in Anthes (1958: 19): discussed in Montserrat (2000: 72).
8. Said (1989: 207).
9. *Recorder*, 9 July 1926.
10. Petrie (1932: 249–50).
11. Private letter written by Breasted: Larson (2010: 107).
12. Quoted in Krauss (2008: 49).
13. Quoted in Wilhelm (2016: 23). The letter and protocol were made public following the 1998 DOG centenary celebrations, which prompted an exploration of its extensive archives. Güterbock's letter, written in 1924 more than a decade after the division but soon after the display of the bust in Berlin, highlights the controversy that was already surrounding the discovery and display.
14. The legal details of the division are discussed in Urice (2006: 142).
15. Quoted by Krauss (2008: 52).
16. The stela is now in the collection of Cairo Museum: JE 44865.
17. Quoted by Krauss (2009: 20).
18. Quoted ibid.
19. Quoted by Krauss (2008: 47).
20. Quoted by Savoy (2012: 454).
21. Perrot and Chipiez (1884: 244).
22. Readers old enough to recall the 1972 Tutankhamen touring exhibition in London will remember a similar, nationwide interest in ancient Egypt backed up by press reports, books, lectures, radio and television

programmes. A whole generation of professional Egyptologists was inspired by that tour.

23. Borchardt (1913: 43, Plate 19).
24. Parzinger (2016: 149).
25. *Der Mann, der Nofretete verschenkte: James Simon, der vergessene Mäzen.* Wedel's documentary is summarised by Tony Paterson, *Independent*, 4 December 2012.
26. FO 371/2724. Quoted by Desplat (2016).
27. FO 141/589. Quoted by Desplat (2016).
28. For details of the discovery of the tomb of Tutankhamen, and subsequent events, see Tyldesley (2012).
29. Huppertz et al. (2009: 236).
30. Borchardt (1923).
31. Hutton (1785: 110). This phenomenon is not confined to museums: it has long been realised that the more paintings an art gallery houses, the less time visitors will spend looking at any particular painting in that gallery. See, for example, Robinson (1928).
32. See, for example, Casey (2003: 2–3): 'Museums do not just gather valuable objects but make objects valuable by gathering them. The museum is able to produce cultural knowledge by organising how the materials it authorises are seen – by controlling the Gaze.'

6 The German Queen

1. Quotations taken from B. Rohnan, German Foundation Refuses to Return Nefertiti Bust, *Reuters Science News*, 24 January 2011.
2. Quoted and discussed in Schneider (2014) and Krauss (2009: 22).
3. FO 371.12388. Quoted by Desplat (2016).
4. FO 371.13878. Quoted by Desplat (2016).
5. Berlin Museum 14145.
6. Breger (2006: 291).
7. Cited ibid. (289). Breger notes that in the same month *Berliner Morgenpost* reported that the bust stood alone and unvisited.

8. Simon's letter is discussed in Carola Wedel's television documentary *Der Mann, der Nofretete verschenkte: James Simon, der vergessene Mäzen*, and is quoted by Kischewitz (2012: 474).

9. George Rothschild, pers. comm., 2016.

10. Our information about this thwarted attempt to return the bust comes from an interview given by von Stohrer to *Journal d'Égypte*, published on 23 and 29 October 1948. Its accuracy is discussed in Krauss (1991b).

11. The 'fascist Akhenaten' is discussed by Montserrat (2000: 108–13).

12. Tiy overshadows Nefertiti in almost all early accounts of Akhenaten's reign, because the evidence relating to Nefertiti was discovered later. For example, Janet Buttles, writing the *History of The Queens of Egypt* in 1908, was only able to accord Nefertiti six pages (1908: 131–6).

13. Petrie (1894: 40).

14. KV 46. Davis (1907).

15. FO 371.53375. Quoted by Desplat (2016).

16. Farmer (2000: 84).

17. FO 371.53375. Quoted by Desplat (2016).

18. FO 371.63051. Quoted by Desplat (2016).

19. Figures cited by Soltes (2006: 71).

20. Here we are concerned with ancient Egyptian artefacts alone. The wider subject of works of art acquired as souvenirs of imperialistic campaigns stretches from works seized by the Romans to works seized by the Third Reich. See the discussions in Merryman (2006).

21. Arguments over the return of the Nineteenth Dynasty funerary mask of Ka-nefer-nefer from the St Louis Art Museum make interesting reading. There is evidence to suggest that this mask was stolen from the Egyptian Antiquities Organisation some time between 1952 and 1959, and the US government has been willing to return it, but the museum has raised a successful legal challenge to the government's attempts to seize the mask.

22. Krauss (2008: 52).

23. From Napoleon to the Nazis: The 10 Most Notorious Looted Artworks. *Guardian* online, 13 November 2014.

24. George Rothschild, pers. comm., 2016.

25. Quoted in Wilhelm (2016: 25).

26. Ibid. (24).

27. *Der Spiegel* interview with Hermann Parzinger quoted in Schneider (2014).

28. Urice (2006: 165).

29. Siehr (2006: 114).

30. *The Graphic*, 26 March 1927: 496.

31. Zahi Hawass to D. Wildung, 2007: quoted in Ikram (2011: 148).

32. Quoted in *Der Spiegel* online, 10 May 2007.

7 Multiple Nefertitis

1. Kemp (2012: 130).

2. This process was described in Teltscher and Teltscher (1987: 7); quoted in Merrillees (1990: 42–3):

    the director of the Egyptian Museum (Berlin) commissioned her to produce copies of the busts of king Amenophis IV and of Queen Nefertite [sic] and other sculptures excavated at Tell el-Amana [sic]. The special challenge of this commission lay in the fact that Tina was not permitted to remove the originals from their climatically-controlled glass cases and so had to do her measurements 'at a distance'. Stone had been specially shipped from Tell-el Amana for the commission. Tina did not seek to secure legal rights to her copies, and subsequently a series of copies was made from her originals. As a gift, the director invited her to select some antique Egyptian beads.

    It seems unlikely that the Nefertiti bust was in a climate-controlled case when its official replica was made.

3. Historical Replica of Nefertiti: After a Model by Tina Haim. Press release issued by Gipsformerei of the Berlin State Museums December 2013. It is often claimed that a mould taken from the original bust was used to cast the first replicas; this has proved impossible to verify.

4. For example, in 1925 Richard Jenner was allowed to remeasure the bust and make a replica with the ears and uraeus restored. The various models of the bust, and the dates of their sales, are discussed by Dlugaiczyk (2016).

5. Mendonça (2016).

6. The two cast courts in the Victoria and Albert Museum in London, home to an astonishing collection of Italian replica sculpture, are among the most popular galleries in the museum. The history of the cast collection is detailed on the museum's website: www.vam.ac.uk/content/articles/t/the-cast-courts/.

7. Berlin Gipsformerei website: www.smb.museum/en/museums-institutions/ gipsformerei/about-us/profile.html.

8. Information supplied by Dr Carolyn Routledge, curator of Egyptology and archaeology at the Bolton Museum.

9. This theory is promoted by Stierlin (2009) and Ercivan (2009).

10. Petersen (2012: 446–7).

11. *A Convicted Forger Calls Nefertiti's Bust a Fake*. Smithsonian Channel www. youtube.com/watch?v=Cckwn7jN3Ms.

12. The case of the 'Amarna Princess' was covered by local, national and international press as it unfolded. It has been told from the forger's viewpoint in Greenhalgh's *A Forger's Tale* (Allen & Unwin, 2017). The purchase of the statue was funded by various grants and donations, including a substantial grant of £360,767 from the National Heritage Memorial Fund.

13. Krauss (2009).

14. Ägyptisches Museum Berlin: ÄM 14145.

15. Erman (1929: 230) quoted in Krauss (2008: 27).

16. *The Bride of Frankenstein*, directed by James Whale for Universal (1935). *The Rocky Horror Show*, directed by Jim Sharman for Twentieth-Century Fox (1975).

17. Today part of the permanent collection in the contemporary art gallery of the Brooklyn Museum.

18. Wildung (2012: 82).

19. Nefertiti Hack website: http://nefertitihack.alloversky.com/.

20. See, for example, Charly Wilder's article for the *New York Times* of 1 March 2016: Swiping a Priceless Antiquity … With a Scanner and a 3-D Printer.

21. Southern AFH created three Nefertitis, with the first being a study in painting and a test of their ability to reproduce the sculpture accurately in a standard 3D print. The Landis Nefertiti can be seen on www.southernafh. com/ and www.instagram.com/southernafh/.

22. 'Pirate Party' is a name adopted by political groups in different countries. Their political platform embraces civil rights, freedom of information and the reform of copyright and patent law, and they see great potential in the sharing of information without restrictions.

23. 'Michelle' of Southern Artists, Forgers and Hackers, pers. comm., 2017.

24. Wenman (2016) and pers. comm., 2017.

25. Interview with Mike Balzer and Chris Kopak from All Things 3-D, quoted by Wenman 2016.

8 Looking for Nefertiti

1. Akhenaten used the Amarna Boundary Stelae to explain his plan that the royal family be buried at Amarna. Translation after Murnane (1995: 77–8). Discussed in Kemp (2016).
2. Davies (1903–8, II: 36–45). Huya shows what seems to be the same festival, but in his tomb there are only four daughters, and the year is omitted.
3. Discussed in Kemp (2016).
4. Discovered by the Dayr el-Barsha Project, University of Leuven, directed by Harco Willems, and translated by Athena Van der Perre (2012).
5. Although Akhenaten had intended that Nefertiti would be buried in the royal tomb, Meritaten's unexpected death and unanticipated interment in the royal tomb may have prompted a change of plan, with Nefertiti being granted a tomb elsewhere in the royal wadi. See Kemp (2016).
6. Stuart (1879: 74). Stuart had paid a visit to some of the Amarna elite tombs. The royal tomb had not yet been discovered.
7. Loeben (1986). The shabti could have been manufactured in advance of Nefertiti's death; we have no proof that it was used in a burial. Aldred (1988: 229), however, suggests that it would have been inscribed during the embalming period and this would indicate that Nefertiti died at Amarna.
8. Pendlebury (1935: 28–9). For other references to Nefertiti's 'disgrace' see Seele (1955: 168–80).
9. Davies (1923: 133).
10. Consult Harris (1973a, 1973b, 1974). See also Harris (2008).
11. See, for example, Samson (1977).
12. Object number 296b: Reeves (1990: 130–31).
13. This confusing name-based evidence is discussed by Dodson (2009: 27–52).
14. Ägyptisches Museum Berlin: ÄM 14145. TT 192. Oriental Institute (1980: Plate 47).
15. For example, Fletcher (2015: 225):
    However he [Akhenaten] *died, power now lay in the hands of his existing co-regent 'Ankhkheperure Neferneferuaten' – Nefertiti – who now took the new*

name 'Smenkhkara' (c.1338–1336 BC). With her traditional titles written with a female determinative, later dynastic lists indeed acknowledged the existence of a female pharaoh at the end of the 18th Dynasty, a ruler portrayed wearing kingly crowns but with a distinctly female physique.

Fletcher traces the unwillingness amongst Egyptologists to acknowledge the existence of the female pharaoh Nefertiti to a reluctance by the early twentieth-century 'Establishment' to recognise that women were capable of ruling as pharaohs.

16. TT 139. Gardiner (1928).
17. Gabolde (1998: 153–7).
18. Allen (2009).
19. Davies (1903–8, II: 43–4).
20. Davis (1910); Bell (1990).
21. Smith (1910: xxiv; 1912: 53–4).
22. Cited in Engelbach (1931: 116).
23. Harrison (1966: 111); Filer quoted in Tyldesley (2000: 132).
24. Wente and Harris (1992).
25. 'Dr Selim [radiologist Ashraf Selim] noted that the spine showed, in addition to slight scoliosis, significant degenerative changes associated with age. He said that although it is difficult to determine the age of an individual from bones alone, he might put the mummy's age as high as 60.' Quoted in Mystery of the Mummy from KV 55: Zahi Hawass website: www.guardians. net/hawass/articles/Mystery%20of%20the%20Mummy%20from%20KV55. htm.
26. Luban (1999).
27. Fletcher (2004).
28. Hawass et al. (2010).
29. Joseph Thimes, pers. comm., 2015.
30. Reeves (2015). This paper gives useful links to the Factum Arte images.

BIBLIOGRAPHY AND FURTHER READING

Over the past century many hundreds of books and articles of varying degrees of specialisation and accuracy have been published on Nefertiti and her family. Their number grows every year. Traditional, edited, academic resources, some of them long outdated, are being published and republished on the internet, where they may be found alongside more speculative articles, websites and blogs. Occasionally they are joined by research 'published' in the form of a television documentary unsupported by any reference sources. Multiple versions of Nefertiti are now accessible to all who seek her.

The references listed here include the more basic and accessible publications with preference given to those written in English. Many of the works listed include bibliographies that will be of interest to those seeking more detailed information on specific aspects of Nefertiti's life and legacy.

Readers new to the Amarna Period should start their personal research by looking at the Amarna Project website: www.amarnaproject.com. This excellent resource details the ongoing exploration of the ancient royal city of Akhetaten by Professor Barry Kemp, working in conjunction with the Egyptian Ministry of Culture.

All readers will benefit from looking at the beautifully displayed online collections of the Ägyptisches Museum und Papyrussammlung, Neues Museum Berlin, home to the Nefertiti bust: www.smb.museum/en/museums-institutions/aegyptisches-museum-und-papyrussammlung/home.html.

Aldred, C. (1957), Hair Styles and History, *Bulletin of the Metropolitan Museum of Art* 15(6): 141–8.

Aldred, C. (1973), *Akhenaten and Nefertiti*. London and New York, Thames and Hudson.

Aldred, C. (1988), *Akhenaten, King of Egypt*. London, Thames and Hudson.

Allen, J. P. (2009), The Amarna Succession, in P. J. Brand and L. Cooper, eds., *Causing His Name to Live: Studies in Egyptian Epigraphy and History in Memory of William J. Murnane*. Leiden, Brill: 9–20.

Anthes, R. (1958), *The Head of Queen Nofretete*. Berlin, Geb. Mann Verlag.

Arnold, D. (2012), From Karnak to Amarna: An Artistic Breakthrough and its Consequences, in F. Seyfried, ed., *In the Light of Amarna: 100 Years of the Nefertiti Discovery*. Berlin, Michael Imhof Verlag: 143–52.

Arnold, D., ed. (1996), *The Royal Women of Amarna: Images of Beauty from Ancient Egypt*. New York, The Metropolitan Museum of Art.

Ashton, S.-A. (2004), Egyptian Sculptors' Models: Functions and Fashions in the 18th Dynasty, in J. Bourriau and J. Phillips, eds., *Invention and Innovation: The Social Context of Technological Change*, vol. II: *Egypt, the Aegean and the Near East, 1650–1150 BC*. Oxford, Oxbow Books: 176–99.

Assmann, J. (1996), Preservation and Presentation of Self in Ancient Egyptian Portraiture, in P. Der Manuelian, ed., *Studies in Honor of William Kelly Simpson*, vol. I. Boston, Museum of Fine Arts: 55–81.

Baikie, J. (1917), *The Story of the Pharaohs*. London, A. and C. Black.

Baikie, J. (1926), *The Amarna Age: A Study of the Crisis of the Ancient World*. London, A. and C. Black.

Baikie, J. (1929), The Reliability of Egyptian Portrait-Sculpture in the Round and in Relief, in *Great Ones of Ancient Egypt: Portraits by Winifred Brunton, Historical Studies by Various Egyptologists*. London, Hodder and Stoughton: 3–19.

Baines, J. (1985), Theories and Universals of Representation: Heinrich Schäfer and Egyptian Art, *Art History* 8(1): 1–25.

Baines, J. (1994), On the Status and Purposes of Ancient Egyptian Art, *Cambridge Archaeological Journal* 4: 67–94.

Baines, J. (2007), *Visual and Written Culture in Ancient Egypt*. Oxford, Oxford University Press.

Bell, M. A. (1990), An Armchair Excavation of KV 55, *Journal of the American Research Center* 27: 97–137.

Bennet, J. (1939), The Restoration Inscription of Tut'ankhamūn, *Journal of Egyptian Archaeology* 25: 8–25.

Bernal, M. (1987), *Black Athena: the Afroasiatic Roots of Classical Civilisation*. London, Free Association Books.

Blankenberg-Van Delden, C. (1969), *The Large Commemorative Scarabs of Amenhotep III*. Leiden, Brill.

Borchardt, L. (1905), Der ägyptische Titel 'Vater des Gottes' als Bezeichnung für 'Vater oder Schwiegervater des Königs', *Berichte über die Verhandlungen*, Leipzig: 254.

Borchardt, L. (1913), Ausgrabungen in Tell el-Amarna 1912/13, *Mitteilungen der Deutsche Orient-Gesellschaft zu Berlin* 52: 1–55.

Borchardt, L. (1923), *Porträts der Königin Nofret-ete aus den Grabungen 1912/13 in Tell el-Amarna*. Ausgrabungen der Deutschen Orient-Gesellschaft in Tell el-Amarna III. Leipzig, J. C. Hinrichs'sche Buchhandlung.

Breger, C. (2006), The Berlin Nefertiti Bust: Imperial Fantasies in Twentieth-Century German Archaeological Discourse, in R. Schulte, ed., *The Body of the Queen: Gender and Rule in the Courtly World 1500–2000*. New York, Berghahn Books.

Buttles, J. (1908), *The Queens of Egypt*. London, Appleton.

Carter, H. (1933), *The Tomb of Tut.ankh.Amen: The Annex and Treasury*. London, Cassell. Reprinted 2000 with a foreword by Nicholas Reeves, London, Duckworth.

Carter, H. and Mace, A. C. (1923), *The Tomb of Tut.ankh.Amen: Search, Discovery and Clearance of the Antechamber*. London, Cassell. Reprinted 2003 with a foreword by Nicholas Reeves, London, Duckworth.

Casey, Y. (2003), The Museum Effect: Gazing from Object to Performance in the Contemporary Cultural-History Museum. *Cultural Institutions and Digital Technology. ICHIM 03 Paris*: 2–21.

Černý, J. (2001), *A Community of Workmen at Thebes in the Ramesside Period*. Cairo, Institut Français d'Archéologie Orientale.

Challis, D. (2013), *The Archaeology of Race: The Eugenic Ideas of Francis Galton and Flinders Petrie*. London, Bloomsbury.

Davies, N. de G. (1903–8), *The Rock Tombs of el-Amarna* (6 vols.). London, Egypt Exploration Society.

Davies, N. de G. (1923), Akhenaten at Thebes, *Journal of Egyptian Archaeology* 9: 132–52.

Davies, N. de G. (1941), *The Tomb of the Vizier Ramose*. London, Egypt Exploration Society.

Davies, N. de G. (1943), *The Tomb of Rekh-Mi-Re*. New York, Metropolitan Museum of Art.

Davis, T. M. (1907), *The Tomb of Iouiya and Touiyou*. London, Constable.

Davis, T. M. (1910), *The Tomb of Queen Tiyi*. London, Constable. Reprinted 2001 with a foreword by Nicholas Reeves. London, Duckworth.

Desplat, J. (2016), The Nefertiti Affair: The History of a Repatriation Debate. *The National Archives* 16 September 2016: http://blog.nationalarchives.gov.uk/blog/nefertiti-affair-history-repatriation-debate/.

Desroches-Noblecourt, C. (1978), Une Exceptionnelle Décoration Pour 'La Nourrice qui Devint Reine', *Revue du Louvre: La Revue des Musées de France* 28: 20–27.

Dlugaiczyk, M. (2016), Serien-Star Nofretete, in C. Haak and M. Helfrich, eds., *Casting: A Way to Embrace the Digital Age in Analogue Fashion? A Symposium on the Gipsformerei of the Staatlichen Muzeen zu Berlin*. Heidelberg, Artistoricum.net: 163–73.

Dodson, A. (2009), *Amarna Sunset: Nefertiti, Tutankhamun, Ay, Horemheb, and the Egyptian Counter-reformation*. Cairo and New York, American University in Cairo Press.

Dodson, A. (2014), *Amarna Sunrise: Egypt from Golden Age to Age of Heresy*. Cairo and New York, American University in Cairo Press.

Duncan, C. (1995), *Civilising Rituals: Inside Public Art Museums*. Oxford, Routledge.

Eakin, H. (2003), Nefertiti's Bust Gets a Body, Offending Egyptians. *New York Times*, 21 June.

Eaton-Krauss, M. (1981), Miscellanea Amarnensia, *Chronique d'Égypte* 56: 245–64.

Edgeworth, M. (2007), Double-Artefacts: Exploring the Other Side of Material Culture, in V. O. Jorge and J. Thomas, eds., *Overcoming the Modern Invention of Material Culture*. Journal of Iberian Archaeology (special issue) 9/10: 89–96.

Engelbach, R. (1931), The So-Called Coffin of Akhenaten, *Annales du Service des Antiquités de l'Égypte* 31: 98–114.

Ercivan, E. (2009), *Missing Link der Archäologie*. Rottenburg, Kopp Verlag.

Erman, A. (1929), *Mein Werden und Mein Wirken. Erinnerungen eines alten Berliner Gelehrten*. Leipzig, Quelle and Meyer.

Ertman, E. L. (1976), The Cap-Crown of Nefertiti: Its Function and Probable Origin, *Journal of the American Research Center in Egypt* 13: 63–7.

Ertman, E. L. (1992), Is There Visual Evidence for a 'King' Nefertiti? *Amarna Letters* 2: 50–55.

Exell, K. (2008), Ancestor Bust, in W. Wendrich, ed., *UCLA Encyclopedia of Egyptology*: http://escholarship.org/uc/item/59k7832w.

Farmer, W. I. (2000), *The Safekeepers: A Memoir of the Arts at the End of World War II*. Revised and prefaced by K. Goldman. Berlin and New York, Walter de Gruyter.

Fletcher, J. (2004), *The Search for Nefertiti: The True Story of a Remarkable Discovery*. London, Hodder and Stoughton.

Fletcher, J. (2015), *The Story of Egypt*. London, Hodder and Stoughton.

Gabolde, M. (1998), *D'Akhenaton à Toutânkhamon*. Lyons, Université Lumiére-Lyon 2.

Gardiner, A. (1928), The Graffito from the Tomb of Pere, *Journal of Egyptian Archaeology* 14: 10–11.

Gardiner, A. (1961), *Egypt of the Pharaohs*. Oxford, Oxford University Press.

Goldwasser, O. (2010), The Aten is the 'Energy of Light': New Evidence from the Script, *Journal of the American Research Center in Egypt* 46: 159–65.

Gombrich, E. H. (1972 [1950]), *The Story of Art*, 14th edn. London, Phaidon.

Green, L. (1992), Queen as Goddess: The Religious Role of Royal Women in the Late-Eighteenth Dynasty, *Amarna Letters* 2: 28–41.

Hall, E. S. (1986), *The Pharaoh Smites His Enemies: A Comparative Study*. Munich, Deutscher Kunstverlag.

Hardwick, T. (2010), A Group of Art Works in the Amarna Style, in S. H. D'Auria, ed., *Offerings to the Discerning Eye: An Egyptological Medley in Honour of Jack A. Josephson*. Leiden, Brill: 133–51.

Harrell, J. (2014), Comments on a New Nefertiti Statue and its Place of Origin, *Horizon: The Amarna Project and Amarna Trust Newsletter* 15: 8–9.

Harris, J. R. (1973a), Nefernefruaten, *Göttinger Miszellen* 4: 15–17.

Harris, J. R. (1973b), Nefertiti Rediviva, *Acta Orientalia* 35: 5–13.

Harris, J. R. (1974), Nefernefruaten Regnans, *Acta Orientalia* 36: 11–21.

Harris, J. R. (2008), Apropos Nefertiti(2): Smenkhkara Resartus. *Papyrus* 28(2): 1–7.

Harrison, R. G. (1966), An Anatomical Examination of the Pharaonic Remains Purported to be Akhenaten, *Journal of Egyptian Archaeology* 52: 95–119.

Hawass, Z. et al. (2010), Ancestry and Pathology in King Tutankhamun's Family, *Journal of the American Medical Association* 303(7): 638–47.

Hill, M. (2011), From the Archives, *Horizon: The Amarna Project and Amarna Trust Newsletter* 9: 6–8.

Hodgkinson, A. K. (2013), *Royal Cities of the New Kingdom: A Spatial Analysis of Production and Socio-economics in Late Bronze Age Egypt.* Unpublished PhD Thesis, University of Liverpool.

Hoving, T. (1978), *Tutankhamun: The Untold Story.* New York, Simon and Schuster.

Huppertz, A. et al. (2009), Nondestructive Insights into Composition of the Sculpture of Egyptian Queen Nefertiti with CT, *Radiology* 251(1): 233–40.

Hutton, W. (1785), *A Journey from Birmingham to London Comprising a Description of the Most Interesting Objects of Curiosity to a Visitor of the Metropolis.* London, Pearson and Rollason.

Ikram, S. (2011), Collecting and Repatriating Egypt's Past: Toward a New Nationalism, in H. Silverman, ed., *Contested Cultural Heritage: Religion, Nationalism, Erasure, and Exclusion in a Global World.* New York, Springer Science and Business Media: 141–54.

Illerhaus, B., Staude, A. and Meinel, D. (2009), Nondestructive Insights into Composition of the Sculpture of Egyptian Queen Nefertiti with CT and the Dependence of Object Surface from Image Processing: www.ndt.net/article/ndtnet/2009/illerhaus.pdf.

Johnson, W. R. (1998), Monuments and Monumental Art under Amenhotep III: Evolution and Meaning, in D. O'Connor and E. H. Cline, eds., *Amenhotep III: Perspectives on his Reign.* Ann Arbor, University of Michigan Press.

Jomard, E.-F. (1818), *Description de l'Égypte, Antiquités, Descriptions*, vol. II. Paris.

Kemp, B. J. (2012), *The City of Akhenaten and Nefertiti: Amarna and its People.* London, Thames and Hudson.

Kemp, B. J. (2016), The Amarna Royal Tombs at Amarna, *Akhetaten Sun: Newsletter of the Amarna Research Foundation of Denver, Colorado* January.

Kemp, B. J. and Stevens, A. (2010), South Tombs Cemetery 2010: The Objects: www.amarnaproject.com/documents/pdf/STC-2010-objects.pdf.

Kischewitz, H. (2012), The Thirties – Trouble With Nefertiti, in F. Seyfried, ed., *In the Light of Amarna: 100 Years of the Nefertiti Discovery*. Berlin, Michael Imhof Verlag: 474–8.

Kozloff, A. P. and Bryan, B. M. (1992), *Egypt's Dazzling Sun: Amenhotep III and his World*. Cleveland, The Cleveland Museum of Art.

Krauss, R. (1983), Der Bildhauer Thutmose in Amarna, *Jahrbuch Preussischer Kulturbesitz* 20: 119–32.

Krauss, R. (1986), Der Oberbildhauer Bak und sein Denkstein in Berlin, *Jahrbuch der Berliner Museen* 28: 5–46.

Krauss, R. (1987), 1913–1988: 75 Jahre Büste der NofretEte/Nefret-iti in Berlin, 1 Teil. *Jahrbuch Preussischer Kulturbesitz* 24: 87–124.

Krauss, R. (1991a), Nefertiti – A Drawing-Board Beauty? The 'Most Lifelike Work of Egyptian Art' is Simply the Embodiment of Numerical Order, *Amarna Letters* 1: 46–9.

Krauss, R. (1991b), 1913–1988: 75 Jahre Büste der NofretEte/Nefret-iti in Berlin, 2 Teil. *Jahrbuch Preussischer Kulturbesitz* 28: 123–57.

Krauss, R. (1995), Akhetaten: A Portrait in Art of an Ancient Egyptian Capital, in J. M. Sasson, ed., *Civilizations of the Ancient Near East*. New York, Charles Scribner's Sons: 749–62.

Krauss, R. (2008), Why Nefertiti Went to Berlin, *KMT* 19(3): 44–53.

Krauss, R. (2009), Nefertiti's Final Secret, *KMT* 20(2): 18–28.

Kruchten, J.-M. (1992), Un Sculpteur des Images Divines Ramesside, in M. Bronze and P. Talon, eds., *L'Atelier de l'Orfèvre: Mélanges Offerts à PhD Derchain*. Leuven, Peeters: 107–8.

Larson, J. A. (2010), *Letters from James Henry Breasted to His Family, August 1919–July 1920*. Cairo, Oriental Institute Digital Archive 1.

Lefkowitz, M. R. and Rogers, G. M., eds. (1996), *Black Athena Revisited*. Chapel Hill, University of North Carolina Press.

Lepsius, K. R. (1849–58), *Denkmäler aus Aegypten und Aethiopien* (12 vols.). Berlin.

Lichtheim, M. (1973), *Ancient Egyptian Literature*, vol. I: *The Old and Middle Kingdoms*. Berkeley, University of California Press.

Lichtheim, M. (1976), *Ancient Egyptian Literature*, vol. II: *The New Kingdom*. Berkeley, University of California Press.

Loeben, C. E. (1986), Eine Bestattung der grossen Königlichen Gemahlin Nofretete in Amarna? Die Totenfigur der Nofretete, *Mitteilungen des Deutschen Archäologischen Instituts Abteilung Kairo* 42: 99–107.

Luban, M. (1999), *Do We Have The Mummy of Nefertiti?*: www.oocities.org/scribelist/do_we_have_.htm.

Luban, M. (2015), *My Quest for Nefertiti*. Ogden, Pacific Moon Publications.

Manniche, L. (2012), *The Akhenaten Colossi of Karnak*. Cairo, American University in Cairo Press.

March Phillipps, L. (1911; revised 1914), *The Works of Man*. London, Duckworth.

Martin, G. T. (1989), *The Royal Tomb at Amarna II: The Reliefs, Inscriptions and Architecture*. London, Egypt Exploration Society.

Matthes, O. (2007), Copying Nefertiti. *Horizon: The Amarna Project and Amarna Trust Newsletter* 2: 10.

McGuiness, K. (2015), Drag Queen: The Liminal Sex of the Bust of Queen Nefertiti, *Eugesta* 5: 1–13.

Mendonça, R. (2016), Plaster Cast Workshops: Their Importance for the Emergence of an International Network for the Exchange of Reproductions of Art, in C. Haak and M. Helfrich, eds., *Casting: A Way to Embrace the Digital Age in Analogue Fashion? A Symposium on the Gipsformerei of the Staatlichen Muzeen zu Berlin*. Heidelberg, Artistoricum.net: 95–105.

Merrillees, R. S. (1990), *Living with Egypt's Past in Australia*. Victoria, Museum of Victoria.

Merryman, J. H., ed. (2006), *Imperialism, Art and Restitution*. New York, Cambridge University Press.

Millet, N. B. (1981), The Reserve Heads of the Old Kingdom, in W. K. Simpson and W. M. Davis, eds., *Studies in Ancient Egypt, the Aegean and the Sudan: Essays in Honor of Dows Durham on the Occasion of His 90th Birthday, June 1, 1980*. Boston, Museum of Fine Arts: 129–31.

Montserrat, D. (2000), *Akhenaten: History, Fantasy and Ancient Egypt*. London, Routledge.

Moran, W. L. (1992), *The Amarna Letters*. Baltimore, Johns Hopkins University Press.

Moser, S. (2006), *Wondrous Curiosities: Ancient Egypt at the British Museum*. Chicago, University of Chicago Press.

Murnane, W. J. (1995), *Texts from the Amarna Period in Egypt*. Atlanta, Scholars Press.

Murray, M. (1949), *The Splendour That Was Egypt*. London, Sidgwick and Jackson.

Nims, C. F. (1973), The Transition from the Traditional to the New Style of Wall Relief Under Amenhotep IV, *Journal of Near Eastern Studies* 32(1/2): 181–7.

O'Connor, D. (2001), Eros in Egypt, *Archaeology Odyssey* 4(5): 42–51.

Oriental Institute (1980), *The Tomb of Kheruef: Theban Tomb 192*. Chicago, Oriental Institute.

Paglia, C. (1990), *Sexual Personae: Art and Decadence from Nefertiti to Emily Dickinson*. New Haven and London, Yale University Press.

Parzinger, H. (2016), Remodelling Shared Heritage and Collections Access: The Museum Island Constellation and Humboldt Forum Project in Berlin, in B. L. Murphy, ed., *Museums, Ethics and Cultural Heritage*. Oxford and New York, Routledge: 141–61.

Patmore, P. (1826), *A Guide to the beauties of the British Museum: being a critical and descriptive account of the principal works of art contained in the Gallery of Antiquities of the above national Collection; with an appendix, presenting a general summary of the contents of each room*. London, J. M. Kimpton.

Pendlebury, J. (1935), *Tell el-Amarna*, London, Egypt Exploration Society.

Perrett, D. (2010), *In Your Face: The New Science of Human Attraction*. London, Palgrave Macmillan.

Perrot, G. and Chipiez, C. (1883), *A History of Art in Ancient Egypt*. Paris, Hachette.

Petersen, L. (2012), Nefertiti in Focus: The First Photographs of the Nefertiti Bust, in F. Seyfried, ed., *In the Light of Amarna: 100 Years of the Nefertiti Discovery*. Berlin, Michael Imhof Verlag: 445–51.

Petrányi, Z. (2003), *The Body of Nefertiti*. Brochure to accompany the exhibition in the Hungarian Pavilion, 50th Venice Biennale.

Petrie, W. M. F. (1894), *Tell el-Amarna*. London, Methuen.

Petrie, W. M. F. (1932), *Seventy Years in Archaeology*. London, Sampson Low, Marston.

Phillips, J. (2004), How to Build a Body Without One: Composite Statues from Amarna, in J. Bourriau and J. Phillips, eds., *Invention and Innovation: The Social Context of Technological Change*, vol. II: *Egypt, the Aegean and the Near East, 1650–1150 BC*. Oxford, Oxbow Books: 200–14.

Pollinger Foster, K. (2008), The Eyes of Nefertiti, in M. Ross, ed., *From the Banks of the Euphrates: Studies in Honor of Alice Louise Slotsky*. Winona Lake, Eisenbrauns.

Preziosi, D., ed. (2009), *The Art of Art History: A Critical Anthology*, 2nd edn. Oxford, Oxford University Press.

Redford, D. B. (1984), *Akhenaten: The Heretic King*. Princeton, Princeton University Press.

Reeves, N. (1990), *The Complete Tutankhamun: The King, the Tomb, the Royal Treasure*. London, Thames and Hudson.

Reeves, N. (2001), *Akhenaten: Egypt's False Prophet*. London, Thames and Hudson.

Reeves, N. (2015), The Burial of Nefertiti? Amarna Royal Tombs Project, Occasional Paper 1: www.academia.edu/14406398/The_Burial_of_Nefertiti_2015_.

Robins, G. (1986), *Egyptian Painting and Relief*. Princes Risborough, Shire.

Robins, G. (1999), Hair and the Construction of Identity in Ancient Egypt, c.1480–1350 BC, *Journal of the American Research Center in Egypt* 36: 55–69.

Robinson, E. S. (1928), The Behaviour of the Museum Visitor, *Publications of the American Association of Museums* 5.

Roeder, G. (1941), Lebensgrosse Tonmodelle aus einer altägyptischen Bildhauerwerkstatt, *Jahrbuch der Preussischen Kunstsammlungen* 62(4): 145–70.

Said, E. (1989), Representing the Colonized: Anthropology's Interlocutors, *Critical Inquiry* 15(2): 205–25.

Samson, J. (1973), Amarna Crowns and Wigs, *Journal of Egyptian Archaeology* 59: 47–59.

Samson, J. (1976), Royal Names in Amarna, *Chronique d'Égypte* 51: 30–38.

Samson, J. (1977), Nefertiti's Regality, *Journal of Egyptian Archaeology* 63: 88–97.

Samson, J. (1985), *Nefertiti and Cleopatra: Queen-Monarchs of Ancient Egypt*. London, Rubicon Press.

Sanchez, S. (1987), Nefertiti: Queen to a Sacred Mission, in I. van Sertina, ed., *Black Women in Antiquity*. New Brunswick, Journal of African Civilizations: 49–55.

Savoy, B. (2012), Futurists, Bow Your Heads! Amarna Fever in Berlin, 1913/14, in F. Seyfried, ed., *In the Light of Amarna: 100 Years of the Nefertiti Discovery*. Berlin, Michael Imhof Verlag: 452–9.

Schäfer, H. (1986 [1919]), *Principles of Egyptian Art*, 4th rev. edn., ed. E. Brunner-Traut, trans. J. Baines, foreword by E. H. Gombrich. Oxford, Griffith Institute.

Schneider, P. (2014), *Berlin Now: The Rise of the City and the Fall of the Wall.* London, Penguin Books.

Seele, K. C. (1955), King Ay and the Close of the Amarna Age, *Journal of Near Eastern Studies* 14: 168–80.

Seyfried, F. (2011), Die Büste der Nofretete: Dokumentation des Fundes und der Fundteilung 1912/13, *Jahrbuch Preussischer Kulturbesitz* 46: 133–202.

Seyfried, F. (2012), The Workshop Complex of Thutmosis, in F. Seyfried, ed., *In the Light of Amarna: 100 Years of the Nefertiti Discovery.* Berlin, Michael Imhof Verlag: 170–86.

Shaw, I. (2004), Identity and Occupation: How Did Individuals Define Themselves and Their Work in New Kingdom Egypt?, in J. Bourriau and J. Phillips, eds., *Invention and Innovation: The Social Context of Technological Change*, vol. II: *Egypt, the Aegean and the Near East, 1650–1150 BC.* Oxford, Oxbow Books.

Shaw, I., ed. (2000), *The Oxford History of Ancient Egypt.* Oxford, Oxford University Press.

Siehr, K. G. (2006), The Beautiful One Has Come – To Return, in J. H. Merryman, ed., *Imperialism, Art and Restitution.* New York, Cambridge University Press: 114–34.

Silverman, D. P., Wenger, J. W. and Houser Wenger, J. (2006), *Akhenaten and Tutankhamun: Revolution and Restoration.* Philadelphia, University of Pennsylvania Press.

Smith, G. E. (1910), A Note on the Estimate of the Age Attained by the Person Whose Skeleton Was Found in the Tomb, in T. M. Davis, ed., *The Tomb of Queen Tiyi.* London, Constable. Reprinted 2001 with a foreword by Nicholas Reeves. London, Duckworth: xxiii–xxiv.

Smith, G. E. (1912), *The Royal Mummies.* Cairo, Catalogue Général des Antiquités Égyptiennes du Musée de Caire.

Soltes, O. Z. (2006), Politics, Ethics, and Memory: Nazi Art Plunder and Holocaust Art Restitution, in E. A. King and G. Levin, eds., *Ethics and the Visual Arts.* New York, Allworth Press: 65–88.

Stevens, A. (2006), *Private Religion at Amarna: The Material Evidence.* Oxford, Archaeopress.

Stierlin, H. (2009), *Le Buste de Néfertiti: Une Imposture de l'Égyptologie?* Gollion, Infolio.

Stuart, H. W. V. (1879), *Nile Gleanings Concerning the Ethnology, History and Art of Ancient Egypt*. London, John Murray.

Sweeney, D. (2004), Forever Young? The Representation of Older and Ageing Women in Ancient Egyptian Art, *Journal of the American Research Center in Egypt* 41: 67–84.

Teltscher, H. and Teltscher, B. (1987), *Tina Wentcher 1887–1974: A Centennial Exhibition McClelland Gallery July 26–August 30*. Melbourne, McClelland Gallery.

Thompson, K. (2012), New Forms of Composition – Composite Statues, in F. Seyfried, ed., *In the Light of Amarna: 100 Years of the Nefertiti Discovery*. Berlin, Michael Imhof Verlag: 164–9.

Troy, L. (1986), *Patterns of Queenship in Ancient Egyptian Myth and History*. Uppsala, Acta Universitatis Upsaliensis.

Tyldesley, J. (1996), *Hatchepsut: The Female Pharaoh*. London, Viking.

Tyldesley, J. (1998; revised 2003), *Nefertiti: Egypt's Sun Queen*. London, Viking.

Tyldesley, J. (2000), *Private Lives of the Pharaohs*. London, Channel 4 Books.

Tyldesley, J. (2006), *Chronicle of the Queens of Egypt*. London, Thames and Hudson.

Tyldesley, J. (2010), *Myths and Legends of Ancient Egypt*. London, Viking.

Tyldesley, J. (2012), *Tutankhamen's Curse: The Developing History of an Egyptian King*. London, Profile Books. Published in the US as *Tutankhamen: The Search for an Egyptian King*. New York, Basic Books.

Urice, S. K. (2006), The Beautiful One Has Come – To Stay, in J. H. Merryman, ed., *Imperialism, Art and Restitution*. New York, Cambridge University Press 135–66.

Van der Perre, A. (2012), Nefertiti's Last Documented Reference (for now), in F. Seyfried, ed., *In the Light of Amarna: 100 Years of the Nefertiti Discovery*. Berlin, Michael Imhof Verlag: 195–7.

Van Dijk, J. (1995), Maya's Chief Sculptor Userhat-Hatiay: With a Note on the Length of Reign of Horemheb, *Göttinger Miszellen* 148: 29–34.

Vandenberg, P. (1978), *Nefertiti: An Archaeological Biography*, trans. R. Hein. London, Hodder and Stoughton.

Wedel, C. (2005), *Nofretete und das Geheimnis von Amarna*. Mainz, Von Zaben.

Weigall, A. (1922), *The Life and Times of Akhenaton*, rev. edn. London, Thomas Butterworth.

Weigall, A. (1927), The Beautiful, One-Eyed Nefertiti, *The Graphic* 26 March: 496.

Wenman, C. (2016), The Nefertiti 3D Scan Heist is a Hoax: https://cosmowenman.wordpress.com/2016/03/08/the-nefertiti-3d-scan-heist-is-a-hoax/.

Wente, E. F. and Harris, J. E., eds. (1992), *An X-Ray Analysis of the Royal Mummies*. Chicago, Chicago University Press.

Wildung, D. (2012), *The Many Faces of Nefertiti*. Berlin, Hatje Cantz.

Wilhelm, G. (2016), Nefertiti Was Not Abducted, *Nile Magazine* October/November: 19–25.

Wilkinson, J. G. (1837), *The Manners and Customs of the Ancient Egyptians*. London, John Murray.

Wilkinson, J. G. (1847), *Murray's Handbook for Travellers in Egypt*. London, John Murray.

Willems, H. (1998), The One and the Many in Stela Leiden VI, *Chronique d'Égypte* 73(146): 231–43.

Williamson, J. (2015), Alone Before the God: Gender, Status, and Nefertiti's Image, *Journal of the American Research Center in Egypt* 51: 179–92.

Winckelmann, J. J. (1764), *The History of Ancient Art*, vol. I, trans. G. H. Lodge (1873). Boston, James R. Osgood.

Zivie, A. (2013), *La Tombe de Thoutmes; Directeur des Peintres dans la Place de Maât*. Toulouse, Caracara Editions.

LIST OF ILLUSTRATIONS

9. The painted and inscribed stela, part of a household shrine, chosen by Inspector Gustave Lefebvre in place of the Nefertiti bust. Photo: Getty images

10. The discovery of the 'life-sized colourful bust of queen' in the ruined Amarna workshop of the sculptor Thutmose, 6 December, 1912. Photo: bpk/ Vorderasiatisches Museum, SMB

11 a, b, c, d, e: A modern Nefertiti emerges from a block of Portland limestone. Photos: Frank Tyldesley

12. Little Warsaw: The Body of Nefertiti (2003). Photo: Lenke Szilagyi © Little Warsaw

13. Fred Wilson's 1993 *Grey Area*. Photo: © Fred Wilson, courtesy Pace Gallery

14. Isa Genzken's 2012 *Nofretete*. Photo: Courtesy Galerie Buchholz, Berlin/ Cologne/New York © DACS 2017

15. The Samalut roundabout Nefertiti. Photo: Twitter

While every effort has been made to contact copyright-holders of illustrations, the author and publishers would be grateful for information about any illustrations where they have been unable to trace them, and would be glad to make amendments in further editions.

INDEX

Page references for notes are followed by n